Call Me Puke

A LIFE ON THE DIRT CIRCUIT

Thanks
Puke
·13

Call Me Puke

A LIFE ON THE DIRT CIRCUIT

A MEMOIR

Mark Sieve

TWO HARBORS PRESS
MINNEAPOLIS MN

Two Harbors Press
212 3rd Avenue North, Suite 290
Minneapolis, MN 55401
612.455.2293
www.TwoHarborsPress.com

ISBN - 978-1-935097-62-4
ISBN - 1-935097-62-8
LCCN - 2009928288

Book sales for North America and international:
Itasca Books, 3501 Highway 100 South, Suite 220
Minneapolis, MN 55416
Phone: 952.345.4488 (toll free 1.800.901.3480)
Fax: 952.920.0541; email to orders@itascabooks.com

Illustrations by Wayne Walstead
Cover Design and Typeset by Jenni Wheeler

Printed in the United States of America

This book is for Mr. Radio

CONTENTS

FOREWORD

I HAVE A WEAKNESS for showbiz partnerships. I was raised watching Laurel & Hardy, Burns & Allen, Abbott & Costello, Martin & Lewis, Wayne & Schuster, and later the Smothers Brothers. But until I met Mark and Joe as Puke & Snot in 1975, at the Minnesota Renaissance Festival, I'd never seen a professional comedy team in person. In the midst of the costumed parades and confounded bagpipes, there was the one outstanding show – an event, really.

It was pure, naked theater. Two men, no scenery, no lights, no amplification, not even a stage. Just voices, faces, bodies, swords, writing, and charisma. You'd hear Puke & Snot bellow insults at each other in the middle of some dusty, empty path, and ten minutes later you'd hear hundreds of people, stopped in their tracks in transports of merriment.

To someone like me, who had come up in magic with the idea that the tricks and visual effects were the show and the performer was just the delivery system, Puke & Snot were startling. Their show wasn't about what they did. It was about what they *were*.

Festivals are full of hippies. They paint stars on their faces. Their shows are paced like pottery-making. They smoke pot and live in tents. Penn and I bought a tent but, after one night in it, we moved to a motel. We didn't want dirt, dope, and drumming.

We wanted show biz. And that's what Mark and Joe were. They played the period stuff ironically, bouncing their own all-Americanness off the antique language. Nobody at their show – neither performers nor audience – was actually pretending to be in Merrie Olde. This was real. And beyond the *show*, these boys had the *biz* part down, too; they were the top-earning act on the circuit.

For some reason Puke & Snot took a shine to us. Maybe it was because we liked anachronisms, too. I used a flashlight in my act, and Penn incited applause by asking the audience to imagine Farrah Fawcett-Majors being beaten to death with baseball bats.

Puke & Snot and Penn & Teller hung together and talked music and money and theater and sex. We scoffed at the costumed goat the festival called a "unicorn." Mark gave sound advice: At Renaissance Faires, avoid coffee. It will ruin your day, since the sanitation is only marginally better than the 14th century.

In 1978 Penn and I (with our musicological colleague Wier Chrisemer) lucked into a long run in San Francisco with our three-man show, *Asparagus Valley Cultural Society*, and discontinued festival work. Then in 1981, Penn and I ended that run to launch our stage play, *Mrs. Lonsberry's Séance of Horror*. It was going to change magic and theater forever. It flopped and all of a sudden we were starting over. In 1982 we were back in the woods of Minnesota doing shows every weekend. Puke & Snot were there too—by now so popular they packed the largest stages at every show.

On weeknights, Puke & Snot were booked in clubs, and they invited us to share the bill (as they gently put it – we were actually opening for them) at the Comedy Cabaret in Minneapolis. It was our first non-Renfest gig as "Penn & Teller" and started us on a new kind of material.

In this book, Mark will tell you about the P&S&P&T collaboration on *The Hanging of Mortimer Faust*, our dream of a festival attraction that could *make money without us even being there (!)*. But, being a modest man, Mark won't tell you why Puke & Snot became part of your heart when you saw them.

It's because under the shouts and swaggers, under the jokes and bits and insults, you felt between these two great actors a deep, true partnership, so palpable it made your skin feel warm, no matter how dank the Minnesota dusk.

Teller
February 6, 2009

AFTER THE FOREWORD

LOOKING AT THE EMPTY STAGE, just hours before the first performance, I began to question myself. Have I lost my mind? Am I about to risk my career on a pair of edgy comics in tights? I had seen and been thoroughly entertained by Puke & Snot at Renaissance Faires. But would Disney audiences, expecting the nutritional mother's milk of entertainment, appreciate the rambunctious, bawdy humor they were about to see?

I envisioned standing before my boss' desk where a pile of complaint letters hid him from view. Only his voice would be heard, "Hedrick, you're fired."

But I shook it off, determined to expand the Disney entertainment palette, too long a cadre of marching bands and dancers with pom poms. I could feel the audience was ready and that Puke & Snot would scratch their itch. Their off-beat talents would also help me convince the more-starchy Disney execs that the time for change had come.

Fortunately for me, Mark and Joe played it perfectly. Night after night, the audiences erupted with laughter. And so I was able to spend the next eighteen years successfully introducing new forms of entertainment to Disney audiences all over the world. Does the Disney Company owe its entertainment renaissance to Puke & Snot? Opinions may differ. Let's just say they were the canaries in the coal mine.

~ *Stephen Hedrick, author, former producer Disney Creative,*
  Orlando

PREFACE

ON ONE OF OUR MANY adventures where Joe and I talked some company into flying us to an expensive resort to entertain their agents and employees, I was enjoying a sunset dinner at a beautiful restaurant high above the town of Charlotte Amalie on St. Thomas in the Virgin Islands. The moon rose perfectly over the ocean, the warm Caribbean breeze rustled the table cloth, the wine was exactly right.

I put down my glass, leaned back and said to my dinner date, "Why is it that whenever I find myself in a spectacularly romantic setting like this, I look across the table and see you?"

Joe belched magnanimously and replied, "Just lucky, I guess."

When Joe died suddenly in August of 2008, the laughter took a respectful pause. We had always known *The Puke & Snot Show* could live and prosper and entertain without us; we had rehearsed and trained other actors to work festivals successfully in Maryland,

Kansas City, Boston, and Pittsburgh. I had directed college actors in a Puke & Snot-styled script at Disney World. As long as there was chemistry and a friendly antagonism between them, good actors would make it work.

I called John Gamoke, an old friend who had performed as a Snot "clone" at festivals as recently as 2007. An accomplished stage and film actor and musical-comedy veteran, John understands what makes this shtick click and has the chops to handle it. He was between jobs and impulsively accepted my invitation to spend a few days rehearsing to step out onstage the following Saturday at the Minnesota Renaissance festival, where people had watched Joe and me work together for thirty-four years. Brave man.

The first two days of rehearsal, I struggled. I couldn't hear Joe's voice. I kept trying to get John to deliver the lines the way I expected to hear them. Sitting glumly at home that second night, I was on the phone with my son Peter, a talented musician on tour with the Chris Koza band. I told him that I didn't think I could make this transition work. Pete's response flipped a switch somewhere in the deep recesses of my brain.

"Dad," he said, "The music is there, you just have to learn how to play it."

I went to rehearsal with John the next morning and began to listen to *his* music and respond to it. His was undeniably different from Joe's version, the one I'd been laughing along with all those years. But it was still good music. Suddenly it became fun again.

Thirty-five years and counting. The show is still chugging along. John and I will try not to peak too early.

1

THE PLAN

If I entered into an agreement with that man,
I would be sticking my head in a moose.
~ Samuel Goldwyn

JIMMY HEGG'S BAR AND GRILL was the central clearing house for the theater scene in Minneapolis in the early spring of 1974. Jimmy held court each night, dressed always in a rumpled dark-blue suit and perched on his stool in front of the cash register.

A large, tall, homely, thoroughly lovable gentleman, Jimmy Hegg was a former basketball star at the University of Minnesota and a long-time popular Minneapolis restaurateur. Just to his right, a few feet away, a giant block of fresh Wisconsin cheddar and a basket of crackers sat on the side bar. Every hungry actor in town knew that for the price of a "Jumbo" (a triple shot of the drink of your choice for only a dollar) you could eat free cheese and crackers till closing.

Jimmy loved the theater, loved the actors, the hangers-on, the talented, and the pretenders. He emceed at his own club for years just a few blocks away – Jimmy Hegg's Starlight Club, where on any given night in the fifties and sixties you could see Peggy Lee, Henny

Youngman, Sheckie Green, and a long list of touring Vegas acts who woke up one morning and found themselves in Minneapolis in January doing one-nighters for show-biz-starved Minnesotans.

Now established at his new place on 2nd Avenue and 4th Street, Jimmy ran a scaled-down version of the Starlight Club, where a large proscenium curtain with tasseled ropes completely covered the west wall of the bar. At just the right moment, usually around midnight after the theaters emptied and the place was full of actors, theater habitués, sons of habitués, and a variety of other inebriates, he slid off his stool, strolled to the wall and, with a ringmaster's dramatic flourish, pulled a rope that opened the curtain to reveal a large display of hand-printed placards featuring the names of all the theaters in the Twin Cities.

If you happened to be in a production at any of those theaters, your table responded lustily at the appearance of your little banner. Jimmy delivered a short speech welcoming the theater community, occasionally tossing out a plug for a newly opened show, and then he made the rounds of the tables, dropping one-liners like blessings from a monarch:

"I enjoyed talking to you. My mind needed a rest."

"Next time you pass my house, I'd appreciate it."

"For heaven's sake, leave. And it would be heaven if you did."

The theater scene in Minneapolis was at high tide; the Tyrone Guthrie Theater was already the venerable flagship upon which all of us aspired to serve. I was an actor toiling below decks in steerage at community theaters, trusting that hard work and constant visibility onstage would allow me to rise in good time to the promenade deck. Then, I tortured audiences; now, I torture metaphors.

I was a city dweller for a brief two years, having left the gravel roads and corn fields of small-town Minnesota for the fresh asphalt, bright lights, and promise of the Twin Cities. Directors found me a not unpleasant actor to work with, one with limited skills but abundant energy and exemplary personal hygiene.

I had good hair, my father's large-toothed grin, a single twenty-nine-year-old willing to work for free. I spent my days tending a gaggle of ninth graders at a Minneapolis public school and my evenings honing my craft as an actor on whatever stage allowed me to do my honing.

I had a regular paycheck, a decent apartment, and meaty roles coming my way. Life was good.

So it was there at Jimmy's on 4th Street, lounging comfortably in my favorite red Naugahyde booth, well into my second Jumbo of the evening and feeling terribly creative, charming, and agreeable, that my new friend Joe Kudla presented me with *the plan*.

We had both been working at Theater in the Round, an established Minneapolis playhouse that featured some of the best unpaid acting and directing talent in town—unpaid until Ernie Hudson (soon to co-star in *Ghostbusters*) threatened to boycott the production of *The Great White Hope* in which he was starring as Jack Johnson, saying he needed to buy Christmas presents for his kids. The theater board met, collected some money and the show went on. But that was the first and last time an actor was paid at Theater in the Round.

Joe and I met at the first Minnesota Renaissance Festival the year before, Joe doing a couple of roving street characters, and me playing guitar and acting in a Cricket Theater tent show called *Mitchell-John and Martha*, a twenty-five-minute parody of the Nixon Watergate scandal featuring a rewritten Pyramus and Thisbe scene from Shakespeare's *A Midsummer Night's Dream*. Jane Brody, the now legendary actor, agent, and casting director wrote the script and directed us in our terribly hip theatrical political statement.

My first festival show: the Watergate parody

Joe was telling me a story that happened while he was in character as The Black Knight at the previous year's festival. A Guthrie actor, a Canadian named Ken Welsh, was doing a one-man show at the festival. The Guthrie hired a lot of Canadian actors in the seventies, always a subject of dark discussion around closing time at Jimmy's: "Canadian directors, Canadian actors—coincidence? I think not."

Ken performed soliloquies on request from a small wooden platform placed smartly under a tree near a high-traffic area, gathering small crowds by chatting them up as they walked by on their way to a turkey leg and ale. Ken is known to *Twin Peaks* fans as the multi-faced villain Windom Earle, and much later as the father of Katharine Hepburn (Cate Blanchett) in Martin Scorsese's *The Aviator.* But that day he was just another underpaid actor in the woods outside Minneapolis.

Ken had a scroll hanging from a staff, listing ten soliloquies he was willing to perform. Fifty cents would get you a brief, crisp, professional performance from a real-live Guthrie actor. Someone would request Hamlet's "To be or not to be," for instance. His trusty page trotted out to collect the coins. Welsh cleared his throat impressively and launched into the soliloquy with gusto, overacting just enough to impress the rural patrons, after which he sent the page scurrying around the crowd passing the hat for more money.

It was a good gig; he probably made fifty dollars a day. At one point that afternoon The Black Knight appeared at the back of the crowd, took mock offense to the quality of Welsh's performance and challenged him to a swordfight. Welsh drew his blade, left his tiny stage and advanced on Joe, spouting faux-Shakespearean threats and promising to wreak holy havoc on his person and his family. In the name of artistic integrity, the Black Knight was routed. Big ovation. Ken's page passed the hat again.

Joe's alcohol-fueled idea that night at Jimmy's: Why not re-create that theatrical confrontation eight or ten times a day with two new characters at that fall's Renaissance festival? Write some dialogue, inject some bad puns and silly jokes, work up a good, athletic sword fight and cash in with a well-deserved hat pass?

Two Jumbos later, we had a project. I had never held a sword in my life, but I learned early on that in the theater when someone asked if you could tap dance, you just said, "Of course!" then went off somewhere and learned to shuffle ball change and shim sham shimmy as fast as you could.

I was sharing an apartment at the time with my then best friend Erik Fredrickson, an actor and fight choreographer I met a few years before in summer stock in Alexandria, Minnesota. Erik was known to me then as Fred Miller, but when he applied for an official stage name from Actor's Equity, another Fred Miller had beaten him to it. So he signed up officially as Erik Fredrickson; but from then on was often referred to as "Formerly Fred" by friends who wanted to get under his skin a bit.

Formerly Fred was under contract at the Guthrie and agreed to show me the basics of stage sword combat. He demonstrated the five main target points in foil and epee stage combat, the difference between a parry and a thrust, and the importance of never delivering a blow unless your opponent knew it was coming. He even put me through a few specially designed series of repetitive moves that Joe and I could convert, with a lot of sweat, into something resembling a spontaneous sword fight.

Joe had done some sword work at the Children's Theater Company in a production of *Treasure Island* and was already proficient with a blade. Between the Black Knight and Formerly Fred, I figured by the time the festival came around in August I'd be good enough to challenge Cyrano De Bergerac.

June arrived and we began rehearsals on the shores of Lake of the Isles, one of the many lovely lakes in Minneapolis that convinces Minnesotans in early summer that they made the right choice to stay here through another God-awful endless winter.

Early sword rehearsal: Overacting 101

Hacking and slashing our way through our first ten-minute script, our big idea resembled a professional wrestling confrontation with swords and tights more than it did a comedy performance. But we forged ahead, knowing that no matter how silly we looked and sounded to each other, we wouldn't be the worst act the paying customers would encounter that fall. As long as there was a juggler still learning how to keep his balls in the air, we would be fine. In 1974, *everyone* had a juggling act.

Even more important than dialogue and fight choreography was the name. Marketing was an alien concept, but we instinctively knew that a catchy name could generate curiosity. Wink and Nod, Quip and Rejoinder, The Professor and Stosh, Neil and Bob—"Are those your names, or is that what you do?"—none of these promised comic notoriety. Out of desperation, we borrowed a couple of actual Shakespearean names.

Act 3. Scene II

King Henry IV Part 2 – by William Shakespeare

SCENE II. Gloucestershire. Before SHALLOW'S house.

Enter SHALLOW and SILENCE, meeting; **MOULDY, SHADOW, WART,** *FEEBLE, BULLCALF, a servant or two with them.*

Mouldy and Wart it was. Properly Elizabethan with just a hint of the waggish.

The original premise of the show: Joe accosts a female customer somewhere in the lane and loudly and passionately proclaims his admiration for her. I leap like a tiger to her defense, sword in hand, from a distance of fifty yards, an Olympian leap to be sure, but we are young and elastic, with healthy knees and plenty of cartilage. This will be just enough space for us to gather a crowd of the curious as we close the gap between us, brandishing our weapons and threatening mayhem upon the other.

This was risky on many levels. On slow festival days, there might be few onlookers. Would they think we were drunk and simply ignore us? If we did manage to gather a crowd, could we keep them safely out of range at the onset of the still-uncertain swordplay? Neither of us could afford liability insurance. The dialogue sounded like this:

[From one of the first Puke & Snot shows at the Minnesota Renaissance Festival]

One of our first shows, a few curious onlookers

WART   *Ah! I spy entertainment in yon stout wench. She
               discourses; she gives the leer of invitation. Sometimes
               the beam of her view gilds my foot; sometimes my
               well-sculpted visage...*

MOULDY   *[FROM A DISTANCE] Then does the sun on a
               dunghill shine!*

WART   *What's your name, Sir? Of what condition are you,
               and of what place, I pray?*

MOULDY   *I am a knight, Sir; and my name is Mouldy of the
               Dale.*

WART   *Well then, Mouldy is your name; a knight is your
               degree, and your place the dale: Mouldy shall still be
               your name, a traitor your degree and the dungeon
               your place, a place deep enough; so shall you still be
               Mouldy of the Dale.*

MOULDY   *Are you not Sir Thomas Wart?*

WART   *As good a man as he, Sir, whoe'er I am. Do ye yield,
               sir, or shall I sweat for you?*

MOULDY   *Will you shog off? Or will I have you solus?*

WART   *Solus you egregious dog? . . . I do retort the solus in
               thy bowels, for I can take, and Wart's cock is up, and
               flashing fire will follow!*

MOULDY   *Be gone, good Wart: this will grow to a brawl anon.*

WART   *Then come we to full points here, let etceteras be
               nothing.* [THEY FIGHT]

This was a direct lift from Willie the Bard and, to our astonishment, the first time we launched it, it worked. We could hear people: "Oh look, they're going to fight!" and "Get away from them, son; the shorter one has a sword and he looks demented."

For the record, I am the taller one.

Not surprisingly, our first attempts at dialogue were heavily dependent on Shakespeare. Anachronisms were frowned on at the early festivals, and even though our intent from the get-go was to satirize the whole idea of this fantasy return to Elizabethan England in the woods outside Minneapolis in the late twentieth century, we had to tread lightly or risk banishment from more purist entertainment directors.

It seemed hilarious stuff at the time, and it's obvious to me now peering back through the mists of the seventies that audiences back then were extremely forgiving. Renaissance festivals were fresh, strange – the first faires launched in California in the early sixties. The idea slowly crept eastward as promoters and entrepreneurs realized how easy it was to talk actors into working free on weekends for the promise of an audience, free beer, and a pig roast.

That first season is a blur. Nothing notable stands out in my memory, other than the occasional mortifying spaces in the dialogue that popped up like Banquo's ghost while we tried to get back on track after a sheep ran through the show or a drunk staggered into the circle, loudly seeking his equally sozzled wife.

As actors we were accustomed to hushed and darkened theaters and respectful silence. Now we were working outdoors in the wind and elements with no predetermined stage boundaries and no control over the hooch content of our patrons. This was scary.

On more than one occasion, frustration with me, the audience or his own insecurities completely overcame Joe and he threw down his sword in the middle of the show and stomped off to the pub, leaving me with an audience and nowhere to go except stammer to a conclusion and follow him. The second time this happened I told him that if he ever did it again, he'd be working as a solo act. I was a professional, goddammit, and I expected to work with one.

From that point on, no matter how ugly it got, he hung in there till the end of the show and the smattering of puzzled applause. The following year, with the arrival at the Minnesota Renaissance Festival of a silent magician and a tall, very loud, and aggressive juggler, it got better.

2

BORROWING FROM THE BRITS

You call this a script? Give me a couple of $5000 a week
writers and I'll write it myself.
~ Joe Pasternak

SOMETIME THAT WINTER I was doing promotional comedy appearances for the Cricket Theater with Phil Morton, an old friend of ours whose connection with the brand-new Park Square Theater in St. Paul opened up opportunities for both Joe and me to work there. Phil loved performing bits and pieces of sketches from a popular British comedy revue that took New York by storm in the sixties, written and performed by Peter Cook, Dudley Moore, Alan Bennett, and Jonathan Miller: *Beyond the Fringe*.

Bill Semans, artistic director and founder of the Cricket Theater, asked us to make appearances at civic and corporate functions to generate some visibility for the Cricket. For these occasions, Phil and I did a sketch from *Beyond the Fringe* called "One Leg Too Few," in which I played a theatrical producer auditioning a one-legged Phil for the part of Tarzan. Another of the sketches was entitled "So That's The Way You Like It," their rollicking take on Shakespeare.

Where's all this autobiographical hooey going, you're asking? I'm getting to it; don't get your tights in a bunch. It might be important. We'll find out soon enough. This is not a long book. Besides, if enough people read this, I may never again have to answer the question I get a dozen times a day at festivals: *where did those names come from?*

Phil and I were attempting to adapt "So That's The Way You Like It" to just two actors and it was proving impossible. The sketch is a high-speed farce that purports to present every character type Shakespeare ever wrote in one five-minute piece. At one point, two peasant-types wrapped in burlap dash onstage and exchange exactly two lines:

"It's botched up then, Master Puke?"
"Aye, marry 'tis, Master Snot!"

And they zip off. Gone. They never appear again.

"Great Caesar's Ghost!" I yelled, or words to that effect, slapping my forehead, "Phil! I think I just found the replacements for Mouldy and Wart!"

Puke & Snot debuted the following August in the lanes and open fields of the 1975 festival near Shakopee. Surprisingly, audiences were looking for us and began to gather where they thought we might strike up a show. It was our second season, and already we had "our people." This was encouraging.

One Saturday afternoon, with a large crowd assembling near the maypole in the center of the grounds, anticipating an "improvised" show by the sword guys, I waited. It needed to be just the right moment so that when we started, we'd maximize the number of people we could draw into our little orbit – thereby maximizing the hat pass at the end of the show and maximizing our purchasing power at the pub at the end of the day. It was always about maximizing. Hitch up the tights and gird the loins; it's show time.

Early maximizing, Minnesota path show

Securely hitched and girded, I signaled Joe to begin his verbal siege on a lovely female patron. He did; I forcefully interrupted and we cruised easily through a commanding performance and immediately started maximizing.

As the audience melted away, I heard a voice at my back: "Excuse me."

I turned and found a short, intense fellow with curly brown hair and piercing eyes. "I do a silent magic show. I understand you have a following here, but I'm new to the festival. I was doing my show nearby and I wasn't quite finished when you started. Please be aware you're not the only ones scheduled here."

I apologized, introduced myself and promised I'd eyeball the area carefully the next time to make sure the same boorish behavior wouldn't happen again.

"Thank you," he said. "My name is Teller. Stop by and see my show if you have time."

Teller in Minnesota, still a scary dude

Penn the Big Pussycat

I sat on a bale of hay at his next show and could not believe my eyes when he pulled one hundred steel sewing needles out of an apple, silently swallowed every one of them and pulled them back out of his stomach, *threaded!*

Later Teller introduced us to his friend and fellow-performer, Penn Jillette, who was doing his own unique show on the other side of the grounds.

Penn met the festival's entertainment director at the Ringling Clown College in Sarasota the previous year. We had one oddly memorable meeting with the director to that point and were aware of his unsuitability for the jolly trade of clowning.

The previous summer, responding to a request from the festival to participate in a promotion celebrating the birthday of a local "planned" community, Joe and I found ourselves in full costume early one hot, humid, Saturday morning, trudging down an unnamed, treeless, suburban street with a rag-tag group of festies, some domestic animals, a troop of Cub Scouts, a fire truck, and a high-school marching band. A few curious onlookers peered over their newspapers from their lawn chairs, wondering no doubt what we were celebrating and why we were making all this noise.

We had closed Jimmy Hegg's the night before and were seriously hung over. We were now discussing options: how could we escape this awkward, head-thumping madness before someone we knew saw us? We had been asked to do a twenty-minute show at the end of the parade; but who would know if we skipped it?

Out of nowhere a high-voiced, heavily made up jester was in our face, screeching "Smile! It's a parade! Don't look so glum! It's a celebration! Woo-hoo!!"

I reacted instinctively. "Get away from me, you twit, or I'll stick this sword up your nose." He shot me an evil look and moved on.

A short time later we reached the end of the parade route and were preparing to crank up a show for the dozen or so residents who had gathered. Suddenly the mad clown from the parade stomped up, held out an envelope and barked, "I'm the person who hired you for this event. Here's your checks; now get out of here!"

This was a surprise, to say the least. We had never met the festival entertainment director in person and had never been treated quite like this. I took the envelopes with the two twenty-five dollar checks inside and replied, "Thank you. As soon as we do the show we promised you, there's nothing that would please us more."

He huffed off, but we had the money, did our twenty minutes and held up our end of the bargain.

So the same Hostile Jester had called Penn and invited him to Minnesota to pull on some tights and do some Renaissance comedy and juggling. Penn was a nineteen-year-old street performer. He had recently met Teller, who was teaching Latin in a Philadelphia high school. Teller was also an accomplished magician.

As legend has it, Penn talked Teller into abandoning his dream of a career teaching a dead language to inner-city kids, and they started working together, eventually heading off to the Minnesota festival where they each did four or five shows individually, then combined their talents in one show at the end of the day when the large Penn would use the much smaller Teller as a prop. It was cruel, but very funny.

Penn told Joe after seeing one of our shows, "You guys make me laugh and I don't like *anything*."

I noticed immediately that Penn did one thing better than anyone else we had ever seen: the all-important hat pass. He was aggressive, insistent, and he refused to allow people to leave his show without paying. He and Teller structured their individual shows in ways that built naturally to a big trick and kept the audience right there with them till it was time, literally, for the payoff.

This was important stuff, considering what little we were being paid for our efforts, and the lesson was not lost on Joe and me. Although Penn was much younger, he had the street smarts of a forty-year-old.

Later on, in exchange for teaching me how to beg and still retain some dignity, I taught him how to hit a golf ball. But that's another story.

As time passed and we got to know each other, Penn & Teller and Joe and I became friends and fellow travelers, working at festivals in Toronto, Texas, San Diego, and Denver. Like many talented and driven performers from the early festival days, they soon found a much larger audience, broke into movies and television, and are now perched atop the Las Vegas entertainment hierarchy, the most popular and longest-running show in town. And they work indoors. The bastards.

3

IT'S A RENAISSANCE FESTIVAL, THEY'RE NOT EXPECTING ANYTHING GOOD

I didn't like the play, but I saw it under
adverse conditions. The curtain was up.
~ Groucho Marx

OLD JOKE: Why do some people take an instant aversion to festival performers? It saves time.

Early Renaissance festivals were similar to current ones in one important respect: the level of talent was all over the map. You could find a very bad rope walker sweating hard just to stay on a slack rope strung between two trees, and ... you could round the corner and encounter Avner the Eccentric.

You could watch a bad juggler explaining in tortuous detail how long it took him to learn his craft: "...and please, kids, have some respect for the difficulty of the trick I'm about to perform for your enjoyment ..." and you could stroll to the other side of the grounds and discover the Flying Karamazov Brothers.

A common tactic with some festivals over the years was to stock the stages and lanes with unexceptional entertainment and unremarkable acts that would work for little or nothing, but feature one or two strong, professional shows that were supposed to make customers feel like they hadn't been *totally* ripped off.

Not that there isn't nominal entertainment value in watching a knife juggler stand on the front lip of the stage, warn the audience wryly to "put your children in front of you," then accidentally let one of the daggers fly out into the fourth row as audience members leap out of the way to avoid being skewered. We saw it happen in Seattle.

Not that there isn't unintended hilarity in a husband and wife duo performing a chair-balancing routine at a harvest festival in San Francisco, and at the last moment when the unfortunate woman manages to finally climb atop the highest chair twelve feet off the stage, we hear a huge crash, an audible gasp from the audience, a momentary silence, then a cheerful cry from the husband: "She's all right, ladies and gentlemen! And she's going to try it again!"

Not that there isn't an eerie sense of impending artistic doom in watching a rail-thin actor and a well-upholstered actress perform an interminable and thunderous scene from *Taming of the Shrew* for an audience made up entirely of an unsuspecting family of four on a hot day in Phoenix, and before the poor man and his brood can get to the exit, see them corralled and harassed for gratuities: "Oh please, sir, this is how we make our living; how about a dollar? We need to eat."

But the truly excellent shows we encountered over the years could make you forget all that. At one time at the Minnesota festival in the seventies, you could see The Flying Karamazov Brothers, Avner the Eccentric, Michael Hennessey, The Ochawi Dancers, and Penn & Teller.

Joe and I always felt that Renaissance festivals were the retro vaudeville houses of the early 1900s. According to the old comedians and performers who remember it, vaudeville was always hit or miss. You paid a dime to walk into a darkened theater and watch whoever happened to be in town that week. You could stay as long as you wanted; sometimes you'd see something memorable, often you'd leave wondering how these people ever made a living.

Comedy clubs today are much the same. Anybody who's been to a comedy club in the past twenty years knows you have to sit through two or three "openers" and "features," who are still working on being funny, before you actually get to see the headliner. He's a headliner because he finally figured out what's funny and what's just white noise.

The Great Sven had a classic vaudeville routine that made him a headliner and a good living over a long lifetime on the stage.

The story goes that a young soldier, home from Europe just after V-E day, was strolling the streets of New York City, reveling in his successful return from the war, when he saw a sign above a doorway on a side street in Greenwich Village: "TONIGHT, ONE SHOW ONLY, 8 PM, THE GREAT SVEN, 25 CENTS."

Glancing at his watch and seeing it was almost show time, the soldier decided to see a real New York show his first night home. He walked in, bought a ticket and sat down in one of the few remaining seats. The place was packed. Within moments, the lights dimmed and a voice announced, "Ladies and gentlemen, please welcome the greatest vaudeville performer in history, The Great Sven!"

The place went crazy, people leaped to their feet and the curtain opened, revealing a small table with three walnuts carefully lined up on top of it. From out of the wings walked a withered, gnarled old man in a full-length cape.

With a wave of his hand, he silenced the crowd. A drum roll, and . . . he released a snap. The cape fell to the ground; he was stark naked, his rather impressive member hanging limply in a perfectly positioned small spotlight. Another drum roll, and . . . the Great Sven grabbed the appendage and in three smooth, lightning-quick motions, broke all three walnuts with it. An instant standing ovation.

The curtain closed; the lights came up, and the crowd filed out. The soldier was stunned. An amazing performance, well worth the price of admission.

Fast-forward thirty years. The same soldier is back in New York City, on a sentimental visit to his old post-war haunts. He finds himself in the same neighborhood, glances down a side street and can't believe his eyes: the sign above the doorway reads: "TONIGHT, ONE SHOW ONLY, 8 PM, THE GREAT SVEN, $10"

Unwilling to believe what he's seeing, the soldier enters the theater, pays the ten dollars and sits down in a once-again packed house. The lights dim and a voiceover announces: "Ladies and gentlemen, a big round of applause for the longest-running show in New York, The Great Sven!"

Once again, tremendous applause as the curtain opens, a table with three coconuts on it sits in the center of the stage, and an impossibly shriveled old man steps out in a long cape and, with a commanding wave of his hand, calls for silence. A drum roll . . . the snap is released; the cape falls away; a spotlight hits his inert member . . . another drum roll and, with one smooth motion, the Great Sven grabs the ready weapon and cracks open each coconut, one at a time. Standing ovation as the curtain closes.

The soldier sits there lost in thought, not grasping what seems impossible. As the crowd heads for the exit, the soldier sneaks backstage, sees what looks like a dressing room and knocks on the door.

"Come in."

The soldier pushes open the door and there, sitting on a stool in front of a dressing table, is the oldest man he has ever seen.

"What can I do for ya, sonny?"

The soldier stammers, but finally manages to say, "Sir, I was here in this very theater thirty years ago right after V-E day, and I watched an old man do this same show using three walnuts. It seems ridiculous, because that man was very old back then, but . . . are you the same Great Sven I saw in 1945?"

"I certainly am."

"I can't believe it. How old are you?"

"I'm 110 this month."

"Amazing! Why did you switch from walnuts to coconuts?"

"Son, in my business, the eyes are the first things to go."

Your challenge, should you choose to repeat this story, is to tell it in under a minute. It can be done. But to keep from seriously exasperating your friends and relatives, it *must* be done.

One of Joe's favorite vaudeville stories concerned the legendary Professor Lumberti. Much in demand at vaudeville houses across the country back in the day, the Professor was a one-trick pony. But what a trick!

He walked out onstage with a xylophone, put it down and announced: "Ladies and gentlemen, my name is Professor Lumberti, and I am going to play this xylophone."

A wall of boos would cascade down.

"I repeat; I am going to play this xylophone for your entertainment. I'm going to play 'Listen to the Mockingbird.' It's the only song I know. But I'm going to play it so well, so perfectly, that you will give me a standing ovation when I'm finished!"

More boos, louder and more threatening than ever. The professor picked up the sticks, and as he played the first notes of 'Listen to the Mockingbird,' a curtain opened behind him, revealing an absolutely stunning woman, who immediately began removing her clothes to the music. The applause began, built to a crescendo and, just as the professor hit the final note, her last item of clothing sailed off into the wings.

The audience sprang to its feet in the predicted standing ovation, a big smile appeared on the professor's face and he said, "Thank you! You wanna hear it again?"

It seemed to us that the professor had the perfect act. It had everything: music, comedy, nudity, and brevity. Sadly, over the many years we worked on our little show, we only managed to achieve one out of four. And some days we got shut out.

Jimmy would understand.

4

GROWING UP LUCKY

*What a childhood I had; why, when I took my
first step, my father tripped me.*
~ Rodney Dangerfield

EARLIEST MEMORY: the world was young; I am lying in bed upstairs in my grandparent's house. I am three years old. A sudden commotion downstairs at the front door, celebratory whoops and hollers from my grandfather and my mother, a deep baritone laugh I don't recognize. I jump out of bed and run down the stairs, trying not to trip in my footed blue pajamas. A tall man in an Army uniform is being engulfed by my family. I grab his right leg, hold on tight and yell, "Daddy!"

It is the first time I have ever seen him.

My mother always maintained that I was too young to remember that night in 1945. But she also told me that from the time I was old enough to speak, every time I saw a man in an Army uniform I'd ask, "Daddy?" – a source of amusement to Mom's friends and no little embarrassment to my respectable Irish grandmother, Barbara.

The events of that night echoed eerily in my own adult life forty-three years later when I returned from a summer of touring western Canada with the *Knights of Pythias Circle of Death Family Fun Show*, the name Joe gave our two-man touring comedy act. I pulled up behind my home in South Minneapolis and got out of the car just as the back door of our house opened and my seven-year-old-son Peter raced out through the gate and wordlessly enveloped my leg with his skinny little arms, refusing to let go.

Ellsworth is a tiny railroad town in the southwest corner of Minnesota, built by Irish, Dutch, and German immigrant farmers and laborers, a perfect place to be a child. Long sun-filled summers stretched out endlessly as my friends and I played daily pickup baseball games from dawn to dusk, stopping only when we heard our mother's voices call us in for dinner.

My best friend Duke and I planned and executed exotic adventures: climbing to the top of a grain silo near the rail yard to catch pigeons; jumping on our bikes and pedaling twelve miles to the neighboring village of Adrian, then pedaling straight back again, feeling like we'd just spied on a foreign country and lived to tell about it; spending hot August afternoons swimming naked in a murky sand pit west of town, never telling our parents where we were going, knowing they'd refuse to allow it; waiting till after dark to strip off our shirts, smear ourselves with dirt for camouflage and conduct a night raid on my elementary school, which entailed my making sure the second-floor classroom window was left unlocked that afternoon so when we climbed the brick exterior using the recessed handholds in the bricks the architect thoughtfully provided us, we could gain easy access and roam the pitch-black halls like assassins.

Duke's given name was David, but no one called him that except his parents. Nicknames were important where I grew up. Everyone seemed to have one. Three bachelor brothers worked a farm just south of town; their names were Hen, Turtle, and Rooster Jenkins. Nobody knew their actual names. Our best friends were Bump, Skip, and Mouse. I was to become Frog by the time I left in 1956, a nickname I neither accepted nor acknowledged. One mile south of the city limit was the Iowa border. It was an easy ride to Don Linssen's farm where we hopped off our bikes, waded through the waist-high alfalfa and actually stepped into another state. It was the late 1940s: we were free-range children and our world was large.

Strong women lived here. Great-grandmother Mary Fitzpatrick Hollaren had six young daughters and when her husband died of Bright's disease the county arrived to take her children and place them in foster homes.

A single woman could not be expected to raise daughters without a man in the house; proper homes would be found for them. Mary Fitzpatrick stood firmly in her doorway, the little town rose up behind her, and the authorities backed down. Mary kept her family together. Among those six daughters still living in Ellsworth were my grandmother and three of her sisters, Mamie, Josie, and Lily, the ancient and venerable inhabitants of a small wood-framed house with a coal shed and an outhouse in the back.

Barb married and raised a family of five daughters. Her sisters were my maiden great-aunts. None had married, although Lily came closest when Hap Reilly, the postmaster, dated her years before.

Lily agreed to go for buggy rides with Hap, but only if her cousin May came along as chaperone. Naturally, Hap married May.

So the three maiden sisters bought a house together and lived out their long lives working in stores and homes as clerks and housekeepers to support themselves. Josie started her working life at the age of five, standing on empty peach crates washing dishes for a local cafe.

They walked to mass every day, attended every wedding and every funeral, visited the sick and kept a drawerful of candy in the credenza inside their front door beneath a large, framed print of the thorn-crowned and suffering face of Christ on the Shroud of Turin.

Their house smelled like boiled cabbage and old linen, and it was always the first stop for Duke and me before we'd begin our daily adventures. A pocketful of aunties' candies fortified us against the day's nutritional uncertainties.

Grandmother Barbara married Ernie, a German druggist who invented his own dog-worming pills, smoked King Edwards cigars and helped her produce those five daughters, among them my mother, the petite and lovely Helen.

Independent, smart, ambitious, an excellent dancer at the Saturday night big band dance offs at the Red Roof Ballroom, and rooted firmly in a traditional Catholic faith that trusted first in God and everything would follow properly as it should, Helen was a beautiful brunette with full lips and a tiny waist who fended off five marriage proposals from five sturdy suitors before finally giving in at the age of twenty-four to Ben, the rugged son of immigrant German farmers from a neighboring town who was seven years her senior, a decent trombone player, as good a dancer as she was and more than ready to start his family.

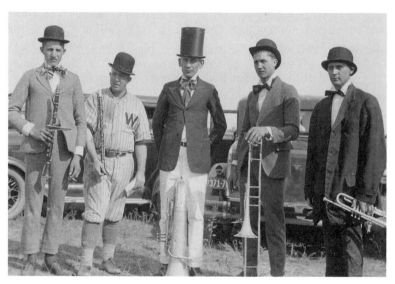

Dad and his trombone. It was all about the hats.

Dad and Mom

Helen's version of their betrothal was that she told Ben if he didn't marry her before he went off to war, she'd be married to someone else when he got back.

They exchanged vows December 30, 1941, three weeks after Pearl Harbor. Dad became the oldest recruit in the county as he prepared to head to Georgia for basic training.

I was born December of the following year, and Dad wasn't allowed to take the train home for the event. A month later, in California and about to be sent overseas, Ben walked into his company commander's office and announced he was going home to see his son.

Dad was a likeable but stubborn guy, his CO told him no leaves were being granted and he'd just have to ship out with the rest of the company and see his child when the war was over. Dad said no, just put me down as AWOL because I'm going home.

The CO blustered and threatened, reminding dad it was wartime and there were serious consequences for leaving the base against orders. Ben shrugged and told him fine; he knew there was a good chance that once he boarded that ship he wouldn't return alive and goldarnit, he wasn't going to leave this earth without meeting his newborn son.

The standoff went on for a few more minutes. The CO swore under his breath, something about "bullheaded Krauts," pulled out a form from his desk, and signed it. Dad headed to the train station.

Helen worked during the war at Silverberg's Ready To Wear in Worthington, keeping up with the rest of the county on the progress of the war and counting and comforting the new widows each month. Ben earned a Bronze Star and a cluster and stayed alive as best he could in the bloody battles with the Japanese in the Philippines.

The Western Union delivery man walked into Silverberg's front door one afternoon and headed straight down the lingerie aisle toward my mother, holding a telegram. All the sales clerks and customers stopped what they were doing and watched. He got within five feet before she fainted and dropped to the floor. It was just a supplier's telegram from Chicago, but those were times when the mere sight of a Western Union uniform struck terror into every woman and child with a husband and father overseas.

After the war, my parents went into business in Ellsworth as soon as my father recovered sufficiently from the malaria he brought back from the jungle. They opened Ben's Café, a little beer and burger joint next to the only bank on Main Street.

I was allowed to play any songs on the juke box I wanted to hear, as long as the customers supplied me with nickels. Mom cooked and waited tables; Dad did the books and worked the front of the house, glad-handing the customers. My parents were charter members of Tom Brokaw's "Greatest Generation," the backbone of the emerging middle class after the War that set an impossible example of hard work and achievement that in later years their children would attempt to emulate.

But Ben's Café was only a steppingstone, their dreams were bigger. Dad put down some money on a building in the next block and began construction, much of it by his own hands, of a movie theater – Ellsworth's first. He poured the concrete, bolted in the rows of seats and installed the massive projectors.

By 1948, the Mark Theater was a sparkling reality, my name in huge steel and neon letters on both sides of the marquee right up there where all my schoolmates could clearly see and resent it.

Ben and Helen named their theater after their oldest child, never thinking that it might set me up for periodic pummelings from the town's young toughs who hated me for having my own building before I graduated from elementary school.

Our family moved out of our grandparents' beautiful stucco home on the south side of town into a two-bedroom apartment above the theater, sharing the second floor with the renters who moved in and out of the four single rooms Dad renovated to supplement the family income.

Dad was now a successful businessman and a popular figure in town, a decorated war veteran who built an entertainment center that overnight became the trendy place to be seen. Someone told him to run for mayor; he did and was easily elected.

I was now an official target, the entitled child with his name on the marquee, his dad the mayor. Across the gravel alley lived Larry, a scary kid a few years older than me who hated me with a single-minded passion, constantly plotting new and artful methods of taunting and torturing me.

An early attempt at musical comedy, Dames At Sea

I dreamed of revenge, but he was pathological, and I didn't want to escalate this unwanted war into something I wouldn't survive. Many years later I was cast in a musical comedy in Minneapolis, and good old Larry showed up as the lead singer/dancer. You could have knocked me over with one of his feather boas. The bully had blossomed.

There were other oppressors. The ironically named Harms brothers would lie in wait for me as I biked to school in the morning, terrorize me with threats, challenge me to fight and, jeering, send me on my way when I refused. This stuff went on for a few years, I stood up for myself as best I could, but I knew I was outnumbered by the barbarians.

It finally all came to a head one winter night when I was eleven. I left the local city hall gym where I had watched a high school basketball game, waved goodbye to Duke and a couple of friends and headed for home.

Shadowy figures appeared between two parked cars as I started across the street. There they were, the two sadistic eighth-grade thugs I knew well and always tried to keep at a safe distance. The son of the local barber, Dickman, and his weasel accomplice, Johnny D.

They were notorious for ambushing the little kids and stealing their pocket change. No one ratted them out because they would thrash you later when you least expected it. They appeared out of nowhere, pinned my arms behind me and—after asking me if I thought I was a big shot and did I know my dad was a sonofabitch—knocked the wind out of me with a couple of perfectly placed gut punches and said go ahead and tell your mom, you crybaby.

I was mortified, struggling to breathe, desperately wanting to defend my father's honor, but knowing resistance would subject me to much worse. I staggered two blocks to our apartment above the theater and, when Mom heard me stumble up the stairs, gasping and trying not to cry, she asked, "What happened?"

I stammered their names and, before I could finish, she was down the stairs and out the door.

She returned a few minutes later, fixed me a hot chocolate and tucked me in for the night, reassuring me that everything was going to be fine; she'd seen to it. It wasn't till the next day that Duke told me she had run across the street to Fischenick's Café where she found the two little hoods perched at the counter eating ice cream.

She grabbed them both by the hair, pulled them off the stools, spun them around and informed them in front of the whole crowd that if they ever touched her kid again she'd break their legs with a baseball bat.

The word went out among the local tough guys that Mrs. Sieve was not to be messed with and, if you value your knees, don't touch her children. From that point on I never worried again about being the mayor's kid. I had a stalwart 110-pound Irish bodyguard.

1953 with my brothers, Dad and bodyguard

*1949 - Dad on opening night,
the Theater of Me*

The Mark Theater was the brand-new family business, and what a playground! Mom met with the film distributors and salesmen every week, armed always with the latest movie ratings from the Catholic Legion of Decency. Dad hand-spooled the latest feature on the editing table upstairs in the projection booth, repairing small tears and defects in each film, taping and splicing until it was ready for that night's showing.

Mom sat on a tall stool in the ticket office in the tiny lobby, selling adult admissions for fifty cents, students over twelve for twenty-five cents, and children for twelve cents.

I happily manned the popcorn machine and the candy counter, bagging and selling popcorn for a dime and Necco Wafers and Beeman's gum for a nickel. I felt like an important cog in the family machine, a valuable contributor who might one day exercise his option as first born and inherit the whole conglomerate, employing my little brothers and sister while I counted the receipts and smoked Cuban cigars.

For now, I was learning the basics of the theater business. The day after each feature I swept out the rows of seats and ran the vacuum cleaner down the thin center carpet while my dad worked upstairs. I was busily cleaning up empty popcorn bags and Black Jack wrappers one afternoon when the overhead lights suddenly went out and the screen was filled with the huge and menacing face of a gigantic gorilla. Enormous teeth bared, it roared out a challenge to the empty theater.

The broom flew out of my hands and I ran for my life upstairs to the safety of my father. "What was that?" I trembled.

"I'm sorry; did I scare you?" He was smiling. "I didn't know you were working down there. That's Mighty Joe Young; he's the star of tomorrow's movie. I was just testing the opening reel."

I watched a few more minutes from the well-lit projection booth before I slipped down the stairs and out into the bright sunshine, away from the nightmarish monster that I knew would haunt my dreams if I ever dared to watch the film.

My parents ran three features a week, the musicals and Technicolor comedies Sunday through Tuesday, the black and white "serious" film noir and detective thrillers Wednesday and Thursday, and either westerns or Abbott & Costello comedies Friday and Saturday. Mom always booked a Warner Brothers cartoon for the Sunday-through-Tuesday crowd; Dad often came downstairs from the projection booth and our little family gathered in the back entrance of the small auditorium, laughing hard at Bugs Bunny, Daffy Duck, Elmer Fudd, Pepe LePew, and Foghorn Leghorn.

Wednesdays and Thursdays featured a Pete Smith short subject or a newsreel, and I always hoped the Friday-Saturday feature was one my parents agreed I was old enough to see, because it was Mom's habit to book the latest Three Stooges short. Even though the Stooges' humor often seemed lost on her, to me it was pure brilliance.

The sound effects, the beautifully timed and choreographed slapstick, and the ridiculous chaos of a Stooges adventure were delicious every time. My dad and I shared a love for that special brand of comedy, and I thought about those early days in the darkened Mark Theater many years later as he stood in the crowd at the Puke & Snot show, his red-faced approving laughter at my own brand of costumed slapstick all I needed to know that yes, by God, this was truly funny stuff. Dad's laughing! To hell with the critics.

Those were exciting, joyful times. The theater was full most nights; even the weekend matinees sold out. My seat in my theater was front row left, on the aisle. I was right on top of the screen, the reason my mother later assumed I needed glasses at the age of nine. I have since learned that sitting close to the action likely had nothing to do with my Magoo-like nearsightedness, but it allowed her to take responsibility for it, which was fine with me. Still, I was the only child in my classroom with glasses. It made me stand out; I was different, and I did not enjoy being different.

Duke and I were in our customary seats one Saturday afternoon for *The Fighting Sullivans*, the 1944 wartime forerunner of the story told in *Saving Private Ryan*. Amid all the tales of personal tragedy in WW II, this emotionally gripping depiction of the Sullivan boys of Waterloo, Iowa, was the most memorable. The five inseparable brothers enlisted together after Pearl Harbor and were all assigned to a battleship that ended up at Guadalcanal—where all five brothers died in action.

When the house lights came up, Duke and I headed wordlessly up the aisle, out the door and down the street. We ducked between the post office and Fusky's grocery, made it quickly to the alley and immediately burst into tears, Duke wailing "Why did they all have to die?"

We were sensitive children, easily affected by a good story well told.

I was able to use admission to the movies as trade bait for free games of pool at Duke's dad's pool hall next door. An afternoon of shooting eight ball on one of his dad's tables was equivalent to one movie ticket and all the popcorn he could eat. I was fascinated with everything about the game of billiards, although it was just pool to us. The glossy, polished, perfectly round, and brightly colored balls, the brushed green felt over the slate tables, the click-clack of balls colliding and disappearing into the leather pockets, the smell of the talcum powder we used to keep our hands dry, all of it.

We played pool often as children. By the time I reached the age of ten I was challenging and beating the old farmers at Fischenick's snooker table. Snooker was more difficult than straight pool. The table was bigger, the pockets and balls smaller, the scoring system more complex. I was proud of my proficiency in this big-person's game and took on all comers.

Duke's father Johnny sold the pool hall in the mid-fifties and assumed ownership of his father's butcher shop and grocery store in the next block.

"Hey," Duke says one bright summer morning, "Let's watch Dad butcher a cow."

Standing behind Lenderts Lockers, we watched a cow unloaded from a truck down a chute and onto the killing floor. Plugging our ears with our fingers so as not to hear the shot from Johnny's 22 rifle that killed it, we hurried around to the side door in time to see Johnny slit the throat, the blood flooding the smooth concrete floor, circling the center drain, then gut the animal, bright slick rubbery intestines spilling out haphazardly, using a longer, sharper knife to skin it, then hang up the glistening carcass on a hook for more knife work. But then we were gone; we'd seen enough.

It was an early education, but the butchering process was never as difficult to watch as the actual killing was to hear.

My 4th grade Montgomery Clift impression

School was two-story, red brick, and Catholic, next door to the church where my parents were married. There were five kids in my class at St. Mary's, and I was later able to say with a straight face that I'd graduated from elementary school ranked second in my class. Tommy Bofenkamp nailed down valedictory honors, but I considered myself a more rounded scholar than he was. I was after all an athlete, a pitcher on the St. Mary's baseball team who could throw hard enough to make Tommy's left hand swell up.

The school was so small that we didn't have a class clown; we took turns. Thank you, Henny. Seriously folks, it was so small that each of the Franciscan nuns who taught there supervised three or four grades in one classroom. My third-grade class shared a classroom with the fourth and fifth grades.

Most days began with mass at the church next door. I learned my Latin prayers and put in my time as an altar boy, attending to the mysteries of the liturgy as Father Redder and Father Scheuring officiated in the traditional Latin rite with their backs to the congregation, so our supplications to God literally needed to pass through them to get to Him.

Our teachers were a memorable lot, originating all the nunnyness you can see onstage today in any of the "Nunsense" styled musicals playing everywhere. My parents worked seven days a week and depended, as all growing Catholic families did in Ellsworth, on those nuns and priests to watch carefully over their kids while they built their businesses and attended to commerce.

We were told repeatedly that if we were ever to get in trouble at school, it would be doubly hard on us when we came home. So it was between that particular rock and the other distinct hard place that I found myself, along with the rest of the kids in grades three, four, and five, in the year of The Terror of Sister Virgana.

Sister Virgana was crazy. We didn't know it at the time; we figured it out many years later. She didn't like kids, a trait shared by some in education who find themselves with a teaching degree, a firm grasp of their subject material, but lacking the most basic prerequisite for the job – a fondness for children.

She meted out harsh physical punishment to those she caught daydreaming or nodding off. Missed homework assignments were a particular sore spot with the demented young woman—for this was not a wizened old nut job we were trying to please, but a strong, youthful sadist who seemed to take great personal satisfaction in discovering that one of her students failed to complete an assignment. Hellish Dickensian retribution followed immediately.

She patrolled the aisles between our little oak and iron desks, observing our work, ready to pounce on the slightest infraction or mistake. One of her most-dreaded methods of getting our attention was to walk up to her chosen prey, stick her fingers in the hair of the offender and twist and pull a large lock out by the roots. She then tossed the little clump of hair on the desk with a cruel and casual "Keep the change."

My fortuitous crew-cut kept me from that harrowing experience. Most often the short-haired boys were jerked out of their seats and stuffed into the good sister's broom closet, the door slammed shut accompanied by her cheery and sarcastic, "Don't let the bogey man get you!"

We often sat in the inky darkness for an hour before she'd open the door and send us blushing to our seats.

One night I sat at my grandmother's dining-room table, a terrified third grader facing baffling arithmetic problems due to be completed the next morning. I was working frantically, tears of frustration streaming down my cheeks, trying to make sense of the numbers and not succeeding. Mom saw me and asked why I was crying.

Mindful of her warnings about "getting in trouble at school," all I could muster was "I can't figure this stuff out." Mom was surprised at how serious a student her oldest child had suddenly become, and told me not to worry, just ask the good sister in the morning and she would certainly explain it clearly. I went to bed with the problems unsolved, praying that overnight I would develop a strong fever that would keep me safe at home for at least another day.

The following morning in class, hunched over my papers, desperately trying to come up with an excuse that might calm the Beast, I heard that familiar threatening voice directed at Tom, one of my fourth grade friends. "Where's your arithmetic paper, Tom?"

Tom was not the brightest light in the room, he was notoriously good-natured, always competing for class-clown honors, but at this moment fully aware he was in big trouble. The required paper was nowhere to be found in his desk or his folders.

"I think I might have thrown it in the waste basket."

The rest of us exchanged ominous glances. Something very bad was about to happen. The Banshee floated out from behind her desk and up the aisle to his desk.

"Stand up," it growled.

Tom got out of his desk on the left side so it was between him and the Awful Presence. Out of nowhere came sister's right fist in a round house punch that caught Tom directly on the nose, lifted him over the next row of desks and threw him flat on his back with a loud crash on the polished oak floor.

Rita, a shy, beautiful sandy-haired girl on whom I had a huge crush, sat right in front of me. Reflexively lowering my head with the rest of the stunned class, I watched a pool of pee gathering at my feet. Rita was definitely frightened.

The Franciscan Fiend had in the meantime walked back to her desk, picked up the heavy metal wastebasket and brought it back to where Tom struggled to his feet, his nose bleeding but a defiant grin on his face. She lifted the wastebasket over her head, turned it over in mid-air, and brought it down violently over his head so that it completely covered the upper half of his body. Trash and paper flew everywhere.

"If it's in there, you'd better find it."

I don't know who finally blew the whistle on her, how she stayed under the parental radar for so long, or exactly when they found out their children had been abused and terrorized for four months, but when we reluctantly returned after the Christmas holiday a stranger, a thin little man, stood behind her desk and introduced himself as a "lay teacher."

He explained that the Wimpled Demon was assigned a position at a rest home in another community. Even at that young age I had visions of old people in wheelchairs being pushed down flights of stairs like Richard Widmark's victim in *Kiss of Death* (now showing at the Mark Theater, once nightly, matinees Saturdays and Sundays).

But she was gone. We looked at each other, not yet comprehending what this meant. Slowly, over a period of days, our little classroom seemed brighter, sunnier, and full of possibility. The witch was dead. Or at least not coming back to torment us. The adults in our lives had risen up, the scales had dropped from their eyes, they had rallied to protect us, and we were free to be kids again!

From that day on, my elementary education was a friction-free gallop through to the ninth grade, with wonderful, caring nuns and priests who took their time, rewarded our work and made us all feel cherished and valued.

Our family grew in size in accordance with the conventional growth patterns of most Catholic families in the fifties, a new addition every two or three years depending on your parent's success or failure at navigating the treacherous waters of the rhythm method. Walking to school one bright March morning in 1950, I saw my

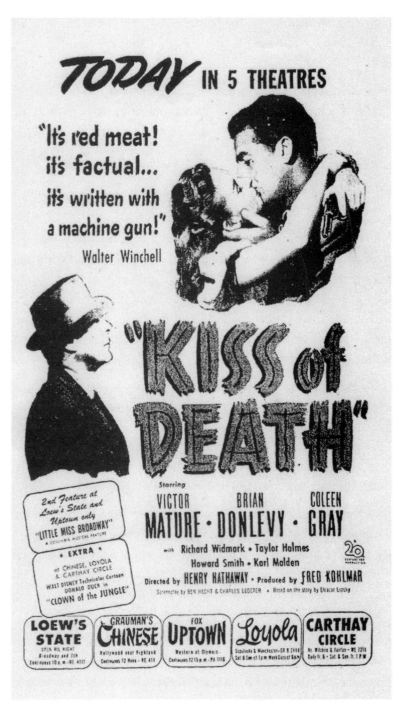

father turn the corner in the family sedan, roll down his window and yell as he passed me, "You've got a new baby brother! His name is Kurt!"

That would make three of us, excellent! My brother Jon had arrived a few years earlier and turned out to be a really fun little guy who made me laugh, even though Grandma Barb made him her immediate favorite to the near exclusion of the rest of her grandchildren. Two more kids, Michael and Katherine Mary, showed up before Mom and Dad decided that four sons and a daughter were just about right, thank you very much.

The movie business was good, seats were full seven nights a week, and my parents were taking every dollar they could spare and paying off the mortgage. This, while an admirable attempt to own their business and be free and clear of debt, would turn out to be a bad decision. An unforeseen and cataclysmic technological development was just over the horizon, about to send a thriving business sliding into bankruptcy.

Black and white television sets started popping up in homes all over town. Ellsworth was one of many farm communities of about five hundred residents that dotted the landscape over southwestern Minnesota. With a good set of rabbit ears, a home anywhere in the county could receive three strong television signals. Within a year the Mark Theater went from full houses to one or two people a night.

I found myself planning homework at my friend Vince's house, never telling my parents that the real reason Vince was my new best friend was that his family owned a TV set where we could gather on Thursday nights and watch *The 64,000 Dollar Question*. Television was a four-letter word in our home above the theater.

It was a life-changing turn of events. They had done everything right, but were about to lose everything they had worked for. My father talked about it years later. In 1954 someone had offered him over fifty thousand dollars for his business, and in less than a year he couldn't even sell the popcorn machine. It would be years before mom and dad would forgive television for what it did to them and finally buy a TV set.

Dad tried a variety of jobs, including a stint selling Fuller Brush products door to door to his rural friends and neighbors. I went with him on his route, but even though he was a natural salesman and people liked him and ordered stuff they probably didn't need, his heart wasn't in it. He was not happy working for other people.

So it was goodbye Stooges, hello Green Acres. By the fall of 1956 my parents packed us all up and moved us to a farm in north central Minnesota where my father could be his own boss and feed his family. I said farewell to Duke and the childhood I'd known, adjusted my glasses and bravely set out with my brothers and little sister to see if we could learn how to milk cows, bale hay, shovel shit and, more importantly, have a good time doing it.

5

NATIONAL INSECURITY

Walter Mondale	*George Bush doesn't have the manhood to apologize.*
George Bush	*Well, on the manhood thing, I'll put mine up against his anytime.*

~ Great Moments in Political Debates

BY 1977 PUKE & SNOT turned an invisible corner and were now gathering large crowds wherever we popped up on the grounds. It was becoming more and more difficult to put Joe up in a tree and have him swing down and land in front of a lovely woman to start the show. People saw us walking around and followed us, anticipating action. Defying all logic and taste, we were a "must see" show. The dialogue reflected it.

SNOT	*Why you tattered prodigal lately come from swine keeping, think not to share with me in glory anymore. Two stars keep not their motion in one sphere.*
PUKE	*Do you imply that there is not room enough here for the both of us?*

SNOT   *In a word...that's correct.*

PUKE   *Well...if we knocked out that wall, put a sofa here, an end table there, couple of lamps...*

SNOT   *Enough! The hour is come to end the one of us, and would to God thy name in arms were now as great as mine!*

PUKE   *I'll make it greater ere I part from thee!* [THEY FIGHT]

Dramatic pause, 1978

It was time to change the approach. Larger crowds meant larger voices were needed; working in a circle meant movement had to be more carefully blocked so the people standing in the back had at least a chance to hear the bon mots we so carefully crafted.

SNOT *I can no longer brook thy vanities.*

PUKE *Then I shall make a river of thy blood.*

SNOT *If so, you shall barge down that river and sink.*

PUKE *Not by a dam site. If you catch my drift.*

SNOT *I catch it sir, but this stream of threats holds no water.*

PUKE *My mind harbors dark thoughts of your impending death.*

SNOT *I shall hold you at bay...you hound...your tide is out.*
      [THEY FIGHT]

PUKE *Somehow I don't like the flow of this....*

Absolutely first-rate. The groans were louder than the laughs. We were determined not to be taken seriously. And the hat pass was less predictable and more profitable.

PUKE *I'm getting hungry. Let's go get some corn.*

SNOT *I'm hungry too. But I can't eat corn. I've got bad teeth. About all I can eat is broth.*

PUKE *Fine. Let's go to a brothel.*

SNOT	*Do you have any money?*
PUKE	*No. Do you?*
SNOT	*No.*
BOTH	*I wonder where we can get some...*

A year earlier, on a sunny Saturday in September, I noticed that a personable, very curious ten-year-old boy named Patrick appeared regularly at our shows, asking us a hundred questions afterwards and offering to carry our swords. He seemed to be auditioning for a page job.

One afternoon he materialized after the show and said, "Hey, see that lady in the wine booth? That's my mom. Wanna meet her?"

I looked at the shop and saw a very attractive woman in a dark-blue dress selling wine to a line of patrons. I suddenly realized that I was indeed very thirsty and a glass of wine would certainly hit the spot. Joe and I had to walk by the shop anyway on our way to our next show, so it certainly wasn't out of my way.

Young Patrick introduced me to his mom; we had a brief conversation, and I left, intrigued with her clear disinterest in the fact that I was an up and coming very funny guy.

This particular wine booth became a regular stop on my ramblings about the grounds. I soon discovered, through careful questioning, that the Lady in the Blue Dress was named Jan; she was happily single, as was I; she worked at a salon at one of my favorite malls, and since I did indeed need a haircut, what a good idea it might be to get one, and soon.

Patrick in his element,
a three sport kid

Lady in the Blue Dress, 1976

Jan and Pete

Peter outside Jan's
booth, 1982

The following week I showed up at the appointed time and when she finished clipping and combing, my hair was stunning. In heartfelt gratitude, I offered to buy her dinner. She carefully accepted, with a reserve and mild skepticism I found challenging.

Fifteen months later on New Year's Eve, Jan, Patrick, and I became a family with three cats and a house in South Minneapolis. In August of 1979, son Peter joined us.

Jan opened a shop at the Minnesota festival where she sold beautiful hand-made children's toys and costume accessories. Pat and Pete learned to juggle and climb Jacob's Ladder. I concentrated on getting funnier.

By this time, the original owner sold the Minnesota Renaissance Festival and moved to Texas, where he had quickly built and opened a Renaissance Festival north of Houston. He asked us if we would consider traveling to his Texas festival at the conclusion of the Minnesota show. "Call me; we'll work out the details. We'd love to have you. We'll put you up off the ground on a stage so the drunks can't get to you."

Another visionary gentleman from Chaska, Minnesota, was planning a new festival near Columbia, Maryland, and had already asked us to come out for a few weekends and help him get his faire launched. We were committed to Maryland, but we also wanted to see what kind of Renaissance festival could possibly exist where the most common Elizabethan exclamation might be "Huzzah, y'all!"

So a show that began as a weekend lark was suddenly a "national" act. At least we liked to think of it that way. I packed up my Renaissance family; Joe led the way, and we drove to Maryland to camp in the woods and see if our little skit traveled well from Minnesota to the east coast.

Jules Smith and his partner Jack Sias leased a public space to mount a festival on the grounds of the Meriwether Post Pavilion near Columbia, Maryland. It was a lovely spot, heavily wooded. The craft booths and tents were dropped here and there among the temporary stages just as a time traveler might find outside London in 1608.

Mr. Smith was an imposing physical presence, 6'8" – and it is rumored, still growing. We first met him when he was selling St. John's bread at a booth at the Minnesota festival; he often wore a red cardinal's cassock. You could see him from far away, like a distant nautical signal.

Jules had a promotional brainstorm: Joe and I were to drive into Washington and crank up a "spontaneous" show in full costume in Lafayette Park, across the street from the White House. Jules would stand nearby holding up an enormous banner that read, "Maryland Renaissance Festival." The lunch time crowd of bureaucrats and diplomats sunning themselves would be hugely entertained and no doubt arrive en masse the following weekend to pay full price for more of the same. It was exceptionally clever.

Everything went according to plan; Joe and I were clanging our swords, generating chuckles, chortles, and more than a few guffaws from a large crowd of onlookers when we saw two uniformed men speaking quietly with Jules. He nodded, immediately walked over, interrupted the show and said, "Let's go. They're kicking us out."

"Who is?"

"The Interior Department. They asked me if I had a permit. I tried to bluff them. I told them I had one in the car from the D.C. police. It didn't work, the Interior Department controls this park and if we don't leave right now we'll be arrested."

It lives in my memory as my first and no doubt last White House performance. We never got inside; but we could see it from where they led us away.

———◆———

The Maryland audiences were delightful and tuned into the language. We were close enough to Washington, D.C., to drop by Congress during the week and visit an old teaching colleague and friend, Bruce Vento. He had left the education business to run for the house seat from the 4th district in St. Paul and was now patrolling the halls of the United States House of Representatives.

Bruce was a state legislator while he was on the faculty with me at Folwell Junior High in South Minneapolis. His reports at teacher meetings of pending legislation never held us spellbound, but he was always knowledgeable and up-to-date on education issues.

That afternoon when my family and I walked into his office, the old Bruce was nowhere to be found. In his place was an impressive gentleman in an expensive gray suit, an excellent haircut, and a firm handshake.

"Who are you and what did you do with my friend Bruce?" I asked.

We talked for a few minutes. He invited us to accompany him to the House floor for an important vote. My son Pat carried his briefcase. In the long walk to the House chamber, we never touched a door. They opened as if by magic, by unseen hands and disembodied voices:

"Congressman, good afternoon!"

"Hello, Congressman!"

"Congressman, good day!"

The smell of power was everywhere. I remember thinking, *yeah, but could he handle a drunken heckler on a Sunday afternoon in the rain?*

By the weekend we were back in the Maryland woods, spewing mock Shakespeare and introducing our new audiences to the poetry in motion that was Puke & Snot.

After one of our scheduled shows, we were approached by a small group of revelers who turned out to be movers and shakers in the Washington political establishment. They were looking for an opportunity to impress Jimmy Carter and the First Family, and they thought Puke & Snot would be just perfect for a special show at the school Amy Carter attended. We agreed.

So back we went in the middle of the week to Washington, once again armed with swords and costumes, wondering how we could adapt this material to fifth graders.

Jules was excited, seeing this little appearance as an opportunity to further establish his festival as a must-see on the local cultural calendar. He drove us to the Sidwell Friend's School in northwest D.C., a private Quaker school where many of the nation's political elite park their children while serving in Congress, the Senate, and the White House. Sasha and Malia Obama enrolled there.

The Secret Service met our car as we pulled up outside the school, introduced themselves with painfully firm handshakes and quickly disassembled our swords and inspected them. Satisfied we weren't there to assault innocent children, they informed Jules that, since they hadn't done a security clearance on him, he had to wait outside.

They escorted Joe and me into the school auditorium where Amy Carter and all her little friends were already gathered for the show. We were introduced as visiting "artists," and the show began. I noticed immediately that in addition to a few teachers, there were three very large, very serious-looking men stationed within a few steps of the auditorium floor where we were performing.

At no time during the first fifteen minutes of the show did any of them laugh or even crack a smile. The kids were hooting and having a good time; these guys were apparently not listening or not amused. I assumed they were Secret Service and working; but this was ridiculous. This was funny stuff and they needed to loosen up. I accepted the challenge, walked over to the nearest agent, looked him in the eye and delivered one of our best punch lines.

He looked right through me. Nothing.

A Sideshow-Bob shudder from me. We picked up the pace, finished the show, met the president's daughter, chatted for a few minutes and left to re-join Jules who was still cooling his heels in the car.

He explained on the way back to Columbia that if either of us had made the slightest move toward Amy Carter during that show, we wouldn't have taken another breath. These secret service guys were trained like Dobermans. And we were carrying swords. According to Jules, who had spent years in Washington, the average length of time a Secret Service agent spent protecting the president and his family was two years. Burnout always happened before that.

Just a year earlier, Amy and her classmates were rehearsing a play to be performed outdoors near an old gazebo that stood on Sidwell school property for generations. Jimmy and Rosalyn, the First Parents, were invited to a special performance and were to sit in a place of honor under the protective roof of the gazebo while Amy and her friends performed on a small stage in front of them. The Secret Service scoured every building and apartment within sight of the gazebo, ensuring that no one could train a rifle on the school yard. The all clear was given, the performance was scheduled.

The day before the show, the roof of the gazebo collapsed in a pile of rotted wood and ancient concrete. Apparently no one had thought to check the structural integrity of the one hundred-year-old building.

Agents were reassigned immediately. People were fired. Tough gig.

6

UNNECESSARY ROUGHAGE

*In his dream he saw thirteen geese, and a fiendish-looking
queen, feverishly eating creamed cheese.*
~ Enunciation exercise for actors

IN MY EFFORTS TO DIFFERENTIATE Puke &
Snot performances from the "expected" garden-variety festival act
featuring either juggling, mime, domestic animals dressed in funny
costumes, fire-eating, or rope-walking, I quite accidentally became a
prop comic at the Minnesota show.

A prop comic is a comedian who makes extensive use of
conventional objects as part of his comedy routine. The name
comes from the stage and film term, "prop" (short for "property"),
which refers to any object handled by an actor in the course of a
performance. Some famous prop comics you may be familiar with
are Carrot Top, Gallagher, Judy Tenuta, Joel Hodgson, and earlier
in his career, Steve Martin. Comedians who are not prop comics
traditionally have little respect for those who are.

I watched a tense confrontation between a prop comic and
a sketch comic one night on the *Tonight Show*. Johnny Carson had
interviewed Gallagher, the notorious watermelon-smasher who

routinely drapes the first four rows of his audiences in large sheets of protective plastic. After a commercial break, Johnny brought out his next guest, Chevy Chase. Carson asked Chase and Gallagher if they knew each other and Chase, his voice dripping with sarcasm, said "Yeah, you're that prop comic, right?"

Gallagher proceeded to tear Chase another comic orifice with a series of hilarious put-downs that reflected the general show-biz knowledge that Chevy hadn't really done much that was actually funny since he fell down a lot doing his impression of Gerald Ford on *Saturday Night Live*.

I had been a fan of Gallagher's since seeing him live at a Fishing and Camping Show at the Minneapolis Civic Center some years before, where he attached a gigantic fishing hook to the back of a life-size child's doll, cast it into a tank of water stocked with fish, and announced that the subject of his lecture would be "Fishing With Children." I was overjoyed when, with no props whatsoever, he verbally reduced the pompous Chase to a quivering blob of unfunny goo in Carson's guest chair.

My point? Ah yes, my point. Prop comics have to be awfully good when they decide to bring "humorous" objects into their act. Their audience is supposedly not as sophisticated as those who are fans of non-prop, or more "intellectual" comics like George Carlin, Robin Williams, and Jerry Seinfeld.

You have no obligation as a reader to retain any of this. No quiz or test will be forthcoming. It only needs to be said in the context of what follows.

In the late seventies, trotting around in tights, with swords and drinking mugs our only props, Joe and I experimented and tried anything that might support our thin scripts, recognizing that the verbal interplay was what carried the show but willing to entertain any idea that might generate laughs. One afternoon I worked my way through a large circle of observers to confront Joe at the beginning of the show, and someone handed me a gigantic carrot to munch on while I engaged Joe in our usual dialogue.

I decided to try to devour the tuber during the course of the show. The resultant cascade of bright orange, half-chewed chunks that ended up all over Joe and the front rows set off gales of laughter that echoed o'er hill and dale. Messy, but definitely a prop whose use we should explore in future shows.

When I was a very young man, I attended my first professional production, a performance of *Richard III* at the Guthrie Theater, starring Hume Cronyn and Jessica Tandy. Several scenes from that play are etched permanently in my memory. One of the most vivid is the scene where the deposed and raging Queen Margaret comes to curse the royals whom she blames for the deaths of her husband and son.

Her speeches are screams in the wilderness of her grief, her curses filled with horrible images. Here she is confronting Gloucester, who she knows killed her family and usurped the throne of her husband King Henry:

> *Stay, dog, for thou shalt hear me.*
> *If heaven have any grievous plague in store*
> *Exceeding those that I can wish upon thee,*
> *O, let them keep it till thy sins be ripe,*
> *And then hurl down their indignation*
> *On thee, the troubler of the poor world's peace!*
> *The worm of conscience still begnaw thy soul!*
> *Thy friends suspect for traitors while thou livest,*
> *And take deep traitors for thy dearest friends!*
> *No sleep close up that deadly eye of thine,*
> *Unless it be whilst some tormenting dream*
> *Affrights thee with a hell of ugly devils!*
> *Thou elvish-mark'd, abortive, rooting hog!*
> *Thou that wast seal'd in thy nativity*

The slave of nature and the son of hell!
Thou slander of thy mother's heavy womb!
Thou loathed issue of thy father's loins!
Thou rag of honour! Thou detested—

The scene was staged so that the mad Queen was in the center of the circle of players, moving freely back and forth, literally spitting curses at them and drenching them with saliva as she clearly enunciated her rage. The audience was also soaked. I thought at the time, "Wow, that's so cool."

Finally I understood why. The act of properly enunciating a Shakespearean speech literally requires the actor to be *fully* orally lubricated. The words must be "spit out," all the T's, P's and S's properly and clearly ejected 'twixt tongue and lips. These dramatic expectorations, so effective in the stage light of a darkened theater, seemed even more lovely when tinged with orange and given some chunky weight.

So the carrot became Puke's signature prop. Audiences soon learned to avoid the front rows when they arrived at our stage show.

One afternoon in front of an overflow crowd at the Crown Stage in Minnesota, we took our bows to a rare standing ovation. It had been a particularly good show with some terrific audience interaction; we went with the flow and felt like we simply nailed it.

I placed my large ceramic mug upstage just before the final sword fight and, during the final bows – in a spontaneous gesture of appreciation – I threw the large remaining carrot high in the air behind me, intending to let it fall harmlessly in the woods backstage. All eyes in the audience followed the trajectory of the partially-chewed missile, until suddenly a huge roar erupted from five hundred throats.

I turned around and saw that I scored an astonishing hole in one, the bottom of the orange projectile sticking straight up out of the mouth of the mug. I looked at Joe; his eyes were saucers.

We turned, bowed and pretended that, yes; this was indeed a normal part of the show, our final "trick." I tried to duplicate that miraculous feat dozens of times in succeeding shows but never came close.

7

AH, WILDERNESS

*If you don't contribute we'll have to hang around
this week and breed with the locals.*
~ Best hat-pass line ever, from The Flaming Idiots,
famous juggling troupe

LIVING ON A FARM is its own education, offering a broad range of learning experiences to an inquisitive fourteen-year-old. Virtually all of life's most important lessons are there to be assimilated: nature's cruelty, birth and death, the vagaries of agricultural capitalism and the uncertain marketplace, love and sex and sweat, and the ultimate redeeming value of hard work.

Making the leap from a privileged child with his name on his own building to a young farm worker learning how to milk cows, chop thistles, and drive a tractor was humbling and exciting. It didn't hurt that our neighbors to the south had six lovely daughters.

Their father, a tall alcoholic named Shorty, beat his wife and his livestock unmercifully. The townsfolk were convinced that her inability to produce a son after six tries drove him to distraction and drink. Men who beat their wives in the late fifties were given a lot of latitude; it was a subject considered out of bounds and "family business."

Our first winter on the farm found me one night tending the farm and my three brothers and baby sister while my parents were out of town trying to secure a loan to pay the taxes. One of our dozen milk cows was close to "freshening," a new term to me. Dad had given me the number of our asthmatic neighbor to the north, Ray Streich, and instructions to call him if I saw any sign that the cow was about to freshen.

Entering the barn that night to do the milking, I saw immediately that the cow in question was lying down, still in her stanchion, with a small wet hoof protruding from her backside. She was breathing hard and well into the birthing process. I ran back to the house, called Ray on the party line we all shared, and croaked, "Get over here fast."

I rushed back to the barn and stood by the laboring cow, telling her everything was going to be fine and to just breathe. The hoof was still in the same position; the cow was working hard but nothing was happening. Finally the top half of the partitioned door opened and Ray the asthmatic farmer appeared, with a white mask covering the lower half of his face.

"I can't come in," he said, "Allergic to the hay dust. But I'll talk you through it."

Talk me through *what?*

"She's having trouble; the head should be coming out first, but it isn't. You'll have to help her. Just grab that hoof and pull."

I looked at the cow. She was suffering, in big trouble. In my brief life to that point I had watched animals die on the killing floor of Duke's father's butcher shop. But I had never seen anything born. On a farm, there are many "first times for everything."

I reached down, grabbed the hoof, leaned back and pulled. Another hoof appeared. I got a grip on both of them and pulled harder. The cow groaned and spit great gobs of saliva. The calf's nose appeared, I pulled as hard as I could, fearing that I'd pull the feet off the baby and hoping please God that I wouldn't. With a final push from mom, the biggest calf I'd ever seen slid out in the straw and blood and manure.

"Open that stanchion, she'll want to get out and clean it."

Ray never actually mid-wifed a calf's birth himself, but he knew how to direct one. I went around to the front of the exhausted animal and released the iron stanchion that kept her in place. She struggled to her feet, turned around, and began licking her newborn.

Ray congratulated me and headed for his car. I milked the cows and watched the new mom finish the clean-up job, feeling older and more responsible than I ever felt in my life. When I proudly related the events of that night to my startled parents, they decided that the calf would be my fourteenth birthday present.

Our old brick farmhouse was basic by any standard, a small kitchen off a ramshackle front porch, old green linoleum through the dining and living rooms and the single bedroom on the first floor.

Little House Near Long Prairie

The dirt root cellar was infested with mice and large, aggressive rats that no amount of D-Con could deter. Each trip to the dungeon by me or my brothers to fetch canned goods or the loose potatoes we stored for the winter was preceded by loud knocking and rapping on the wooden cellar door before entry, the better to let the rodent population know we were coming and to back off and let us do our work.

The house was heated by a small oil stove in the living room. A single metal vent directly above it allowed a modest square of heat to rise into the upstairs bedroom where my three little brothers shared a double bed. My twin bed was set against the wall in a tiny six-by-nine unheated bedroom at the top of the stairs. Winter ice formed early on the unprotected single-pane windows and stayed till spring. On cold January mornings, I came downstairs to find my brothers crouched on the floor behind the oil stove, jostling for space.

These were primitive conditions compared to our former posh digs above the Theater of Me, although we kids made the best of it and often thought of living on the farm as an adventure.

Ben and Helen found ways to make it exciting. We picked chokecherries that grew in thick bushes along our fence line and the family all pitched in to make gallons of chokecherry wine and pints of jelly, which we stored in the dungeon.

On rare summer nights Mom poured fresh cream from that day's milking, some sugar and vanilla into a bucket, packed ice and salt around it, and let us stir up a big batch of ice cream, the best we'd ever tasted. Dad bolted a hoop to the side of the woodshed so his sons could play long afternoons of basketball. Baseball games with a tennis ball required a fly ball to be hit past the garage for a single, off the barn wall for a double, onto the barn roof for a triple and over the barn for a home run. Every animal we owned had a name, including each pig and chicken. We had more pets than anyone we knew.

If it was not exactly Little House on the Prairie, it was our sturdy little family's version; and we made it as much fun as we could.

One night while Dad, brother Jon, and I crouched under our assigned cows, hand-milking them into metal buckets, we heard a strange, low animal sound coming from the direction of the haymow door. Dad grabbed a flashlight and stepped up the ladder to check it out, came back, poured some fresh milk from his bucket into a tin plate and placed it carefully just inside the small access door above us on the haymow floor.

We watched a large pair of cat's eyes appear in the light from the bare bulb near the ladder. When we later checked the metal tin, the milk was gone. The next night, the same low sound from the same place, this time Dad placed the tin of milk on the recessed stone window sill below the haymow door so that whatever was up there had to come down a couple of feet into the barn to get it. We continued milking the cows and watching the access door.

Suddenly the biggest feral cat any of us had ever seen stepped slowly, carefully, one foot at a time, down the ladder step and onto the window sill. It was black with white markings on its head and feet, enormous, bigger than the family dog, at least thirty pounds of wild feline. It eyed us suspiciously as it lapped up the milk, finished and jumped back up into the haymow.

Dad's plan worked. Each night, he placed the milk further into the barn, requiring a bigger commitment from the cat to reach it. Within a week, it was moving cautiously all the way to the front of the barn where we fed the other cats. But it wouldn't allow any of us to approach it. Wherever it came from, its experience with human beings had not been one of mutual trust.

Eventually, after some months of eating our food and drinking the daily plate of fresh milk, Lucifer, that was the name we decided on, made a decision that we were worthy, and we were finally allowed to scratch his head and stroke his back. He began to follow us around the yard and became our favorite farm animal, even earning his living by helping to control the large rat population that inhabited every building on the farm.

Our favorite night-time activity with this amazing beast was to walk with him to the hog house after dark, where we knew dozens of rats would be up feeding on the leftover corn on the dirt floor of the building. We tiptoed up to the building; the cat waited, poised to strike. We flung open the door, flicked on the light and Lucifer pounced as the startled rats scattered. He always managed to kill three or four before the rest escaped into their holes. He seemed to understand that we wanted those rats gone, so he never picked out a single target, he simply killed as many as he could as fast as he could.

It wasn't till years later that we learned how difficult this lifestyle change was for our mother. She was a pharmacist's daughter and had been born and raised in an environment that, while not exactly patrician, was surely free of the daily smell of manure and the sounds of rats racing through the walls of her bedroom at night. Now she was living a very different life, if not on the edge then certainly closer to it than she'd ever been with four young boys and a two-year-old daughter to raise, her family's economic security dependent on weather, her husband's success or failure raising and selling livestock, and her own abilities to find creative ways to contribute to the small income stream.

But she threw herself full force into these new circumstances, planting a half-acre of vegetables and strawberries for canning. She sent me eight miles north to the pickle factory with crates of freshly picked cucumbers and collected the two or three dollars I brought back. She drove into town one day and talked the owners of a local restaurant into letting her bake some pies for them to sell. She did, their customers loved them and she quickly had a job baking up to a dozen fresh pies from scratch each morning, for which she negotiated a rate of sixty cents per pie.

My brothers were at first too young to participate in the day-to-day duties of running the farm, other than small jobs like taking a basket to the henhouse to collect the freshly-laid eggs mom used to bake her pies. So the responsibility of helping Dad do the heavy work fell to me. I was just old enough and big enough for some important jobs that needed daily attention. I was allowed to drive the family car, deliver cans of milk to the local creamery, hook the tractor to heavy equipment like mowers, hay rakes and manure spreaders and feed the few cattle and hogs we housed in the barns.

Dad invited me to watch as he took apart the carburetor on the ancient Allis Chalmers tractor he'd bought at auction. I stood politely as he worked shirtless in the hot sun, his Popeye forearms glistening with sweat as he patiently explained the mysteries of internal combustion. I'd break away as quickly as I could to prop an old mattress against the woodshed, pace off 60 feet 6 inches, and throw baseballs at it for hours.

A ninth grader in the Long Prairie Public School, I was amazed to find I had seventy-one classmates. Our adopted village had twenty-five hundred residents. It was an actual county seat. Huge.

I embraced my new community enthusiastically, making friends quickly. My baseball skills, developed over many summers of day-long games with Bump, Duke, and Skip were quickly discovered by the high school baseball coach and immediately appreciated by the older kids who saw my fast ball as a commodity they could count on in coming seasons.

I became a starting pitcher for the Long Prairie Indians at fourteen, surprising even myself as I took the mound that spring of

On the farm, 1957

THURSDAY, JUNE 1, 1961

Leader

SPORTS

Sieve Strikes Out 19 In No-Hit Game Sunday Night

One of my better outings

1957. Baseball became my entree into Long Prairie's haut monde, a way for me to stand out in the crowd of farm kids and townies.

Other athletes respected what I could do on the field and allowed me to share their space at the local Delite Shoppe, where we downed butterscotch sundaes and ogled the cheerleaders on Friday nights. I was recruited hard by the football coach who coveted my right arm as a quarterback, but I resisted, always aware that the required violence of his sport could easily cost me a broken finger or injured shoulder, thereby making me less effective in the sport in which I was supremely confident I actually had a future.

By my senior year, I became a "prospect," feared by some, respected by most, on my way to a private men's college an hour away where I resumed my relationship with Catholic education.

St. John's University, a Benedictine men's college a mile off Interstate 94 in central Minnesota, yet somehow deep in the woods, is a respected institution on the shores of the fabled Lake Sagatagan, a Sioux word that means, I believe, "Where the hell are the women?"

My parents didn't have the resources to send me there, but it was where they wanted me, a place they felt I would surely find my vocation, which plainly entailed searching my conscience and listening carefully for the call of the Holy Spirit to the priesthood. If there was ever a place in Minnesota where a young man could find the solitude to actually listen to such a call and identify it, St. John's, with not a woman within miles, was such a place.

So with some help from the National Defense Education Act and the money Mom and Dad managed to wring from the family budget each month, I gratefully took up residence in Collegeville the fall of 1960 to begin my four years in the company of men. Tuition was an astounding $1200 for the year, this included classes, food, and a shared dorm room. That was a lot of money.

My parents proudly drove me and a suitcase to St. John's that first night, dropped me at the doors of the quadrangle in the center of the grounds and said goodbye son, be sure to write often. I was only sixty miles from home, but there were to be no long-distance phone bills. If I was lonely or homesick, a four-cent stamp would have to suffice.

I found my room on the third floor of the freshman dorm, dropped off my one bag and made my way to the auditorium where I heard the laughter and din of what sounded like a large crowd enjoying themselves immensely. I entered through a side door and saw hundreds of students and faculty sitting in rows of time-worn wooden folding seats. Onstage was a young man dressed in army greens, grinning and delivering a comic monologue that had the house in hysterics.

I remember nothing about his material, but this kid was *good*. He delivered a line, paused, stared them down and challenged them not to laugh, and the place dissolved. I had found the annual Welcome to St. John's variety show, a tradition where arrival day for freshmen was capped by an evening featuring the best and brightest talent of the incoming class.

The comedian was followed by a crew-cut kid from Arizona with a guitar, who tore it up with a few folk songs. After a closing speech by the dean, we all headed back to our rooms.

That night, sitting at my ancient wooden desk in Room 313, writing my first letter home, I marveled at what I had just seen. What kind of courage did it take to walk out on an empty stage into a spotlight, looking out at hundreds of expectant faces waiting to be entertained? I was a student who rarely raised my hand in a classroom; the fear of being wrong or humiliated was always with me. What kind of transformation would it take for me to be able to do what I had just seen those students do?

The door opened and my new roommate lurched in, slid down onto a wooden chair and introduced himself. He was very drunk and could barely talk.

"Are you all right?" I asked.

"Yeah, I'm fine."

"You look like you're going to be sick."

"Nah ... been drinking beer...never get sick on beer."

With that he slid his chair four feet to the right and emptied his stomach into the sink. I made a mental note to start looking for new roommates the next day.

The theater department was made up of a short, balding barrel of a Benedictine priest named Father Dominic Keller. He had a cigar stub permanently stuffed in the right corner of his mouth and a signed photo of Charles Laughton hanging in the green room, a prized memento from an appearance at St. John's by the movie legend some years before.

Father Dominic directed all the plays at St. John's, most of which ran, of necessity, to heavily male casts: *Twelve Angry Men, Stalag 17,* and the like. On the rare occasions he directed a play that needed women, he recruited a few girls from St. Benedict's, our sister school a few miles away. Those were the productions we all wanted to get involved in, a chance to spend time with people who had higher voices than ours and who smelled so much better than the usual cast in a Father Dominic production.

Later that first year at St. John's I auditioned for and was cast in a few small roles in Shakespeare's *Antony and Cleopatra,* which required me to coat my body with greasepaint, walk like an Egyptian and deliver lines like "I wish you all joy o' the worm."

Father Dominic cast the big-toothed comedian from the talent show as Antony. He was a pre-law student named Bill, exactly my age but with a stage presence, voice, and actor's skills the rest of us had never witnessed outside a movie theater.

I was cast in one more play that first year, as Alfred, one of the three convicts in *My Three Angels*, a romantic comedy made into a popular 1955 movie starring Humphrey Bogart, Aldo Ray, and Peter Ustinov. Bill played the Bogart role. I watched him carefully, absorbing every move he made and marveling at his easy grace and precision onstage.

Many years later, we were to meet again, and the irony and circumstances of that meeting will be visited in a later chapter.

But that spring I made the final cut on the university baseball team as the youngest pitcher on the college staff, so I put away the greasepaint and pursued my main passion for the next four years to the exclusion of further theatrical nonsense. I was going to be a jock, and the gym was to be my home.

Me, Bill the Actor, and Loren in "My Three Angels"

8

WHERE CULTURE
GOES TO DIE

If I owned Texas and Hell, I would rent out Texas and live in Hell.
~ Gen. Phillip H. Sheridan

HOUSTONIANS LOVE THEIR Renaissance festival. Interaction with the actors is a given; the more physical the better. People gathered outside the front gate on weekends at nine in the morning, pulling homemade wagons that unfolded into full bars, complete with ice chests, kegs of beer, and a full selection of vodkas, rums, brandies, and bourbons. This little tradition lives no more at the Houston festival, but in 1979 it was de rigueur.

Bawdy comedy was the rule. Belly dancers were vastly more popular than mimes, and the joust was a twice-daily exercise in Old West cultural history: good guys on horses versus bad guys on horses (no guns allowed).

In this strange land, Puke & Snot were a natural draw. The names alone were enough to promise delicious low-brow entertainment. From the first day we appeared in the lanes, we were an instant curiosity. To us Minnesotans, everything about Texas seemed foreign and decidedly unfamiliar, from the food to the music to the accents.

We attempted to translate these into Midwestern English. One night at a local seafood restaurant, Joe ordered a platter of oysters.

Me: "You ever eaten oysters?"

Joe: "Of course."

When they arrived, he confidently tossed one down, looked at me with one eye slightly crossed and said, "Well, that was interesting."

He reached over and retrieved a small bowl on the table and said "Hey, cole slaw!" One forkful of horseradish later, he declared Texas an enemy to his digestive tract.

There were other peculiarities to deal with. One steamy Sunday afternoon it was show time on the Globe Stage but, before we could begin, we had to solve the dilemma of the besotted four-hundred-pound woman sitting onstage who refused to leave.

Muttering something about losing her husband, she was intractably seated on the floor in the front center of our performing space, oblivious to her surroundings. We tried luring her off with food as bait, but I only had carrots and she wasn't interested.

After ten minutes of bad improv, when calling security finally seemed our only choice, a woman who worked in the ticket office and knew Joe came striding down the center aisle shouting, "Get off that stage! That's my husband you're messing with! Get away from him or I'll kick your ass!"

The poor woman heaved instantly to her feet, mumbled an apology to Joe's friend, and lurched up the aisle. Afterwards, the clever lady who solved our predicament explained that the worst thing a woman could do in Texas was mess with another woman's man. It was an inspired save on her part, and one we could never have guessed might work.

We flew to Texas on weekends in October and November each year till 1985. The first few years I headed for the airport Friday afternoon after a week of teaching, did five shows a day Saturday and Sunday, drove like a psychopath to catch the last flight out Sunday night and be back at my desk Monday morning for another week of teaching the enigmas of English grammar to ninth graders.

It was a heavy work schedule with few days off, but I enjoyed it – even though I knew that on many of those Monday mornings, my students weren't quite getting the teacher their parent's tax dollars were paying for. Mom and Dad had always worked seven days a week; I was carrying on a proud family tradition. The gnawing feeling that all this time away from home and family might someday be a source of regret was easily dismissed whenever I made another mortgage payment. I was a teacher, yes, but also an actor. Actors go where the work is. Simple.

Working with Harpo

The astute owner and promoter of the Texas festival was an architect, a marketing genius, and a renowned party animal. He had built his home near the festival on the bank of a lake he intended to create by damming and diverting a local creek. He had a gigantic hot tub on his deck and a bar-sized men's room urinal built into the wall in his master bedroom. Legend had it that he'd tried to legally change his name to The King but was thwarted by an unsympathetic Texas judge.

His reputation as a not-so-benevolent despot was secured the day he bulldozed an artist's shop when the craftsman in question had failed to make structural improvements in a timely manner. Lawsuits ensued, but The King had made his point. He demanded unswerving obedience and loyalty and ruled his Houston kingdom in a kingly fashion.

The King invited us to a party at his home one festival weekend evening. We arrived as things were well on their way to becoming a future episode of *COPS*. The King handed each of us a beer and ushered us into his office where a huge hand-made graph hung above his desk. This was a marketing tool for tracking food, entertainment, crafts, everything a customer might experience at his festival – the results of feedback from his customers.

He pointed to the long red line that extended from the names "Puke & Snot" and went nearly off the page: "You're the most popular act we've got. Now I have a question: what's your plan?"

I looked at Joe, he shrugged. "Whattya mean?"

"I mean, what's your plan? What's your five-year plan, your ten-year plan? Disney has a ten-year plan; I have a ten-year plan; you gotta have a plan."

"We really don't have one. We're actors. Most actors are happy if they have an eight-week plan."

"Goddammit, that's not good enough. Here's another question. If your father died during this festival, would you go to his funeral or would you honor your contract with me?"

"What kind of question is that?"

One of the women lounging on a leather sofa chimed in, "Oh, leave them alone; that's not fair."

The King was on a mission. "It's a simple question: would you work or would you bury your father?"

"Of course I'd go to my father's funeral; that's a really stupid question."

"I knew you would. You don't have a plan. Where's the loyalty? Nobody gives a good goddamn about a contract anymore. I can't count on anybody, even you guys."

With that, Joe and I put down our beers and headed for the rental car. I remembered Macbeth's line to Lady Macbeth: "O, full of scorpions is your mind, dear wife."

The King had a nest of vipers up there that night.

There was always a sense of danger in Texas, a feeling in the air that bad stuff could happen any time in the jack pine forests of Plantersville. Joe and I talked about this more than once. We noticed on certain weekends that a large crowd of very happy guys showed up en masse at our show, twenty-to-thirty strong. Faces painted, beers in hand, they'd have a good ol' gay Texas time watching the guys in tights spouting double entendres and waving the phallic swords.

I asked them after one of the shows if this was an organized thing or if they were all just friends who met at the festival on a regular basis. One of them confided that it was too dangerous to show up at the festival in twos or threes; they needed the security of a large group, otherwise they feared for their safety from the hard-drinking, pickup-driving hetero Texas boys.

Two of those same good ol' boys took offense to an ad-libbed joke I made at their expense during one hot Saturday show. We watched them make their way from their seats to the side of the stage as the show progressed, and we knew there was going to be trouble as soon as the show was over.

We kept them in sight as we wrapped it up and, as we took our bows, they started up the steps at the side of the stage. Joe grabbed his sword and turned to face them. Nothing was said; we all just stood there for what seemed like an hour. Then a friendly Texas drawl from behind and to their left: "Gentlemen, is there a problem we could hep y'all with?"

It was one of The King's uniformed security boys, packing a large sidearm. He'd been watching our show and saw the faceoff. The tipsy dynamic duo immediately backed down the steps. The trooper smiled at us and escorted them toward the front gate.

We found out later that The King's security force was renowned, not usually this subtle, but extremely effective in dealing with drunks, thieves, and the occasional fight that broke out at the belly-dancer's show. Offenders were sometimes taken behind a fence and disciplined, then walked to their vehicles and sent on their way.

We never saw those good ol' boys again.

Penn called me the previous spring and asked me to talk to a couple of festival owners about booking him and Teller. They had closed a successful run of their brilliant "Asparagus Valley Cultural Society" show in San Francisco and were looking for work. I called The King and, ever the shrewd judge of talent, he hired them. They'd been given a small stage near the entrance to the festival.

Penn & Teller were always "too big for the room," but whoever sat down for one of their shows always left knowing they had seen something special and, of course, they had. The festival had featured another unknown future television star when Harry Anderson, the long-time star of *Night Court*, got his start there a few years before as a fast-talking sleight of hand artist.

Inhognito in Houston

Penn & Teller's backstage was always a popular place to hang out between shows. Joe and I were doing just that one sun-baked Sunday, comparing notes on Texas audiences and telling the latest jokes.

It was always a story-telling competition with Penn, his taste ran to off-beat jokes that a lot of people might find baffling. After Penn's very funny story about a guy who kept bees in a closet in his tiny Manhattan apartment, Joe suddenly launched into the most scatological story I'd ever heard him tell.

He started ugly and became progressively more profane and hilarious. I could tell immediately that he rehearsed it for just this occasion; it was important to top whatever new material Penn brought that week.

Joe's joke went on forever, until finally the talent agent says, "My god, what do you people call yourselves?" The man answers, "The Aristocrats." Penn nearly fell down laughing.

Thirty-three years later, Penn made "The Aristocrats," the movie based on the world's dirtiest joke. A brilliant idea, it features every well-known comedian and comic actor in the country doing his or her version of the joke known as "The Aristocrats." This joke is the professional comedian's yardstick for funny. The premise: a large family auditions their act in front of a talent agent. The act consists of indescribable acts of perversion, debasement, debauchery, and bestiality, which I will not attempt to recount here. The punch line is always the same, but it's the inspired descriptions of the "talent" that determine how well the joke is received. Rent the movie.

When the film was released, Joe and I saw it and I suggested that his "Aristocrats" was still the best. Joe felt Penn should have asked him to do his version that convulsed Penn so many years before. I tried to imagine the movie cutting from Robin Williams' version to George Carlin's version to—Joe Kudla.

He agreed, but I got the feeling he was quietly proud of his primacy as First Aristocrat.

———◆———

One Saturday morning in 1985 we walked in costume through the lobby of the Houston Marriott on our way to the festival. A guy in a cowboy hat, sitting in the lobby, looked up from his paper and said, "You boys goin' to work at the Renaissance?"

Joe: "How'd you guess?"

Cowboy: "You sure it's open?"

He held up the *Houston Chronicle* and on the front page below the fold was the news that The King had fired his long-time food and beverage manager Bobby B that week. There had been a big faceoff on the festival property with news media, police, and photographers in attendance. Punches were thrown.

Apparently it would be tough to get a beer in the kingdom that weekend, not to mention more exotic fare like turkey legs. We set off in anticipation of an interesting day. We were not disappointed.

The festival was in chaos. Bobby B had been running the food and beverage operation there for many years, but someone had convinced The King that Bobby was cheating him out of cash receipts, hiding thousands in coffee cans and burying them around the site. So, the story went, The King walked in with armed deputies as Bobby was counting over seventy thousand dollars in cash on Sunday night and told him to stand up and back away from the table.

The King gave Bobby twenty-four hours to get his trucks

and equipment off the site. It was now the following weekend and thousands of patrons were milling around the festival looking for something to eat and drink. The King had his people making ham sandwiches and selling them for five bucks. He was sending guys in pickups to local liquor stores to buy up all the beer they'd sell him. Bobby B himself was set up in a highway median a mile from the festival entrance selling festival mugs, tee shirts and souvenirs off the back of a truck.

Joe and I had some serious tee-shirt money owed us from the previous weekend, and when we went to The King to get the check, he said briskly, "I don't have your money, Bobby's got your money. Go get it from him."

So we drove out to where Bobby was valiantly trying to get rid of his inventory by shortstopping festival-goers right there in the highway median. He saw us coming and yelled, "I don't have your money, boys. The King walked in with the sheriff and told me to get off the site. Your money was in that pile I was counting. He's got your cash."

"I looked at Joe and said, "Okay, somebody owes us some money; what do you want to do?"

"Let's go get it."

"You know The King won't give it to us."

"Then he can do his festival without us next season, because unless he pays us I'm not working here."

"Good enough."

We met with The King the next day on the deck above the front gate in the shade of a tall pine. He was adamant; so were we. That was my last conversation with The King till I showed up a year later with an idea that I was convinced would fit perfectly into his ten-year plan: we would publicly execute someone at his festival at least once a day. He would offer me ten thousand dollars to make it happen.

9

ALLOW ME TO ASSUME
THAT POSITION

Teaching is, after all, a form of show business.
~ Steve Martin

WHEN I FIRST ARRIVED in Minneapolis in 1971, I had left teaching to become an actor. It took me a month to come to the unsettling conclusion that although I might be good enough to snare an occasional role, I was light years from becoming an actor whom anyone would actually pay to perform. Apparently, this was a profession where you needed a resume. So I played my trump card early and signed up as a reserve teacher in the Minneapolis school system, the perfect job for an unemployable actor: work your day job; then head for rehearsal at night.

I was substituting for a chronically ill English teacher one May morning at Folwell Junior High in South Minneapolis, digging deep into my teacher's bag of tricks to fill in some time with a roomful of over-stimulated eighth graders, when the principal, Byron Schneider, popped in to watch. He stayed awhile, watched me teach my charges, and left.

The next day, back in the same classroom, he visited again, staying longer this time and asking me to stop by his office at the end of the day. I thought at the time that I'd never seen a principal pay such close attention to what happened in a classroom where a reserve teacher was working, but at our meeting that afternoon he got right to the point: he'd talked Cargill, Inc., a local Fortune 500 company, into coughing up one hundred thousand dollars for a three-year program of intensive learning for a small group of selected at-risk students. He wanted to know if I was interested in coordinating and heading up the program and creating a curriculum for it.

It all seemed a bit much. I was, after all, trying to focus on acting, using teaching to pay for that habit. Another steady job? With more responsibility than I'd ever had in a classroom? I asked him if I could think about it; he gave me a week.

The next day I was back in the same classroom and Mr. Schneider and I talked further. He fleshed out what he hoped this program might be: five teachers with diverse backgrounds, no more than a total of thirty-five children, many of them with learning disabilities or serious behavioral problems, field trips into the community, extra-curricular experiences, a role-playing drama curriculum, earth science, civics, and language. The ultimate goal was to keep as many of these potential dropouts in school and learning as long as possible. I would be on full salary with full credit for my experience, three years guaranteed.

It was tempting; it would be challenging. I told him I wanted to pursue my theatrical interests outside of school time; he thought it was a positive and encouraged me to bring as much of that world into his school as I could. This might be fun.

We talked about his background when we had exhausted mine. He was the only Jewish administrator in the Minneapolis system at that time. He reached in his desk drawer and pulled out a black and white photo of more than sixty people at what looked like a family reunion. All the faces had black X's over them, except for one face in the lower-right corner. The photograph had been sent to his mother in this country from her cousin in Austria. Everyone in the photo was killed in the Holocaust but her, the lone survivor from that family reunion that had been celebrated someplace in Europe just before I had been born, with people who looked just like me and my family.

He kept the photograph in his desk so he could always be reminded of the point he wanted to make as an educator and a human being: all those relatives of his had been killed because *the communities in which they lived had allowed trucks to pull up to their neighbor's homes, load up the people and drive them away.*

His point: if their neighbors had known them and cared for them, the men in those trucks couldn't have done that. Communities and towns and villages across Europe would have risen up and stopped it. Until we get to know our neighbors, all of them, from all races and all backgrounds, it could happen again.

This was to be the focus of the program he wanted me to develop for the Minneapolis public schools, a curriculum that valued everyone equally and insisted that we all get to know each other and appreciate our differences.

I said yes, I'll do it.

For the next three years I was given permission to work with four superb teachers in the design and execution of a hands-on education program with the primary goal of turning thirty-five unique and difficult kids into successful students. Our challenge was to utilize private start-up money to create a self-sustaining model. Our wing on the southeast side of the building immediately turned into the liveliest, most dynamic, and most controversial neighborhood in the school.

Controlling and directing this experiment, my team produced wonderful results with children who, up to that point, were serious problem students with little likelihood of reaching graduation day with their psyches intact.

I continued to spend evenings and weekends acting on Twin Cities' stages.

One day at lunch with my best friend on the faculty, Ginny put down her cheeseburger, wiped her mouth with a napkin and said, "Mark, I have to ask you something. I hope you won't take it the wrong way."

"I won't know how to take it until you ask; so fire away."

"Are you gay?" Long pause from me.

"What?"

"I'm sorry, but I thought you should know that most of the faculty is convinced you're gay. I know it's nobody's business but yours, but everybody's gossiping. I certainly don't care one way or the other."

Another pause while I absorbed this. "What do you think?"

"I don't care. I'm only telling you what they're talking about—you're an actor; you wear flamboyant clothes. Sometimes you show up with a necklace or a bracelet ... we never see you with a date at faculty functions."

"Ginny, I'll tell you and no one else. I'm straight. I wear paisley shirts because I like them. I wear jewelry once in a while that I think is cool. I find some nice stuff cheap at Renaissance festivals. I never show up at faculty functions with a date because *why would I impose those awful social events on anyone I actually like – male or female?* But thanks for asking. This is interesting information."

The next faculty meeting I raised my hand and suggested redecorating the faculty lounge in less depressing color schemes.

*I can't believe my fellow teachers
thought I was gay.*

The first play I auditioned for in Minneapolis was an original work at Theater in the Round by Charles Nolte, a former Broadway actor and playwright now teaching at the University of Minnesota. He cast me as a young aide de camp to Mark Frost's Alexander in *Alexander's Death*. Mark was only eighteen, but a talented actor and soon to become an even more gifted writer, gaining notoriety for co-creating *Twin Peaks* for ABC with David Lynch and writing episodes of *Hill Street Blues* and many other television and film projects.

I was offered some good roles at a number of theaters around the Twin Cities, eventually settling in as an occasional director and actor at Mixed Blood Theater, a wonderfully creative environment started and developed by my good friend Jack Reuler. It's the only theater in the Midwest with the mission statement: "Dedicated to the spirit of Dr. King's dream since 1976."

Jack and I met in a production of *Steambath* at Theater in the Round, which lives in my memory as the play with the smallest costume budget of any show I ever did.

I found out many years later that Jack's primary motivation for launching Mixed Blood was the Ernie Hudson situation at Theater in the Round. Jack decided to create a theater that provided minority actors, writers, and directors with a professional forum, a place to work and showcase their talents.

One night in 1982 I got a call from another friend, a bear of an actor named Clive who I eventually directed at Mixed Blood in Ken Lazebnik's *Calvinisms,* a one-man show about Calvin Griffith, the man who brought major league baseball to Minnesota. He asked me to join him at Jimmy Hegg's that night; he was meeting a friend who was in town to promote his TV show.

Clive and his visiting buddy spent the previous summer at the Great Lakes Shakespeare Festival and were getting together for drinks. I stopped by around ten that night, and seated next to Clive was a young actor I had seen in a recent sitcom, *Bosom Buddies.*

"Mark, I'd like you to meet a friend of mine, Tom Hanks."

I sat down and enjoyed a long evening of Jumbos, cheese and crackers, and hilarious conversation with Clive and his friend Mr. Hanks, who to this day still refuses to take my calls. The bastard.

Jack Reuler and me in "Steambath"

10

DEEP THOUGHTS

Stick with me, boys; I'll have you farting through silk.
~ Easy Ed

MINNESOTA HAS FIVE distinct seasons: spring, summer, fall, winter, and baseball. The latter begins anytime between early March and late April, depending on how soon the ground thaws and the snow melts. High school and college baseball teams get an early start on the season by working out indoors in a gymnasium. Rat Hall, the ancient but still serviceable gym where St. John's athletes played their basketball games, was the site of baseball tryouts as the ice on Lake Sagatagan melted and winter sloshed into spring.

I found myself one of dozens of freshman hopefuls working out on the polished hardwood of the basketball court in the spring of 1961. Ground balls hit by assistant coaches shot off the floor like ricocheting bullets; sliding practice was a manly exercise in avoiding floor burns; batting practice took place inside a netted enclosure.

I was encouraged by the number of upperclassmen who took the time to stop by the cage and watch me throw. One senior pitcher warned me that the coach would undoubtedly try to change my throwing motion. I was to listen respectfully and when he left immediately revert to my current windup. It was clear that the veterans had minimal respect for the abilities and baseball knowledge of our coach, Easy Ed.

Easy Ed was a former high school coach from central Minnesota whose main job was to coach basketball. The baseball job was an afterthought. In only one year, Ed had become something of a local Yogi Berra due to his habit of dishing out incomprehensible nuggets of life lessons and Yoda-like wisdom on road trips.

He sired ten children and complained that the Benedictines who ran St. John's expected him to work for subsistence wages and donate the rest of his time to the church. He often shared his experience as a Catholic male, hoping to save us some of the difficulties he underwent: "Before you ask a woman to marry you, boys, always make sure her father has fixed her teeth and bought her a winter coat."

In the middle of a losing streak my sophomore year, he delivered the single most memorable motivational speech on the steps of the dugout any of us would ever hear, just before we took the field to begin a doubleheader against our arch rivals, St. Thomas:

Okay, boys, this is how it works. At the end of the season, all anybody remembers is who ended up in first and who ended up in the cellar. Let's get out there and find a way to get out of the cellar and end up in the forgotten middle. All I want to see is assholes and elbows leaving this dugout. Get out there and BE AVERAGE!

We lost both games.

Despite his obvious shortcomings, I quickly came to value Easy Ed's ability to recognize talent and employ it properly. I made his final cut and became a starting pitcher as a freshman for the second time in my young life.

Wool uniforms...that's me, fifth from the right.

11

TAKIN' IT OFF THE STREETS

*Acting is the most minor of gifts and not a
very high-class way to earn a living.
After all, Shirley Temple could do it at the age of four.*
~ Katharine Hepburn

BY THE EARLY EIGHTIES Puke & Snot were ready
to dive into the stand-up comedy pool. We knew what festivals were
all about; we had even donned English Music Hall costumes and
adapted the show to a series of harvest festivals, playing venues on
the West Coast: San Francisco, Portland, Seattle, and back to the
Midwest: Kansas City and St. Louis.

Agents talked to us about the NACA circuit, a potentially
lucrative college tour that some comedians used to launch their careers
and slide into television (Carrot Top, Sinbad, and Franklin Ajaye). It
would be the mid-eighties before we got involved with NACA.

We worked a benefit at a comedy club in Los Angeles and
spent a few weeks at the Comedy Cabaret in South Minneapolis,
experimenting with the smaller club and lower ceilings that made
swordplay even more adventurous. We'd been getting requests locally
to appear at charity events and found that our brand of comedy
worked nicely at corporate outings, even though our show names

The Professor and Stosh at San Francisco's Harvest Festival

sometimes had to be downplayed or re-invented before the proposal reached the desk of the president for his approval. Puke & Snot over lunch could be a tough sell for those buttoned up business folks unfamiliar with our show.

We accepted one invitation to perform gratis for a small group of retirees in Minneapolis, the Sons of Norway, a fraternal organization representing people of Norwegian heritage in the United States and Canada. Its mission: "to promote, preserve, and cherish a lasting appreciation of the heritage and culture of Norway and other Nordic countries." It sounded harmless, a quick half-hour show, wild applause, and we leave feeling like we've done our bit for charity that month.

We arrived at the appointed time, ready to knock their argyle socks off with our edgy brand of two-man comedy. We waited in a hallway while a pleasant young woman introduced us, and right on cue we burst through the door ready to do the Renaissance rock and roll. What we saw was a roomful of not just old, but *ancient* Norwegians, many of them in wheelchairs, some on oxygen, most accompanied by a private nurse.

Norwegians, for those of you unfamiliar with Minnesota culture, are a reserved lot; even the most effusive of them would never stand out in a crowd at a party; it just isn't done. (Read Garrison Keillor for a closer look at the Minnesota Scandinavian persona) But these nice folks were both Norwegian *and* old; the median age of this audience was somewhere in the high eighties.

Joe and I sensed at once that we needed to match the energy level in the room. We didn't want to be the immediate cause of a heart attack or stroke. The dialogue slowed down; our voices got quieter and the pauses for laughs were shorter.

Because there were no laughs.

Our best material, our biggest laugh lines, got nothing. Oh, we could sense that the breathing got a little quicker from those who we thought might still be awake, but mostly the room was as hushed and still as a Trappist's cell on Good Friday.

We had devised a few verbal cues when we ran into situations like this where the best course of action was to retreat gracefully. This was certainly one of those times. We did fifteen minutes of our best stuff, cut quickly to the end, bowed and headed for the door to what sounded like three people applauding. Probably the nurses.

When we reached the safety of the hallway, Joe leaned against the wall, let out a muttered "God Almighty!" and I collapsed in a chair, giggling in relief.

"Was it us?" Joe asked.

"I have no idea, maybe they just didn't get it – we're in tights, it's a Renaissance show, we probably should have introduced the concept before we started; I don't know. Let's just get some lunch and lick our wounds."

The door opened; it was the smiling face of the pleasant woman who'd introduced us. "Thanks so much, gentlemen. We have a request: would you consider doing another ten or fifteen minutes? They just loved the show."

Silence. Joe looked at me; I stared at her.

Finally I could only ask the obvious. "How could you tell?"

"Oh, they're all pretty old and weak, but they were smiling the whole time, it's the best show we've had here in months."

So we strolled back in to thunderous, smiling silence and ripped through another fifteen minutes. From that day forward, whenever we'd encounter an audience who for one reason or another didn't respond, at some point in the show one of us would yell "Sons of Norway!" as a battle cry and a salute to quiet and reserved audiences everywhere.

The next time you're watching us, if you hear that phrase, it's just us wishing we were funny enough to make you actually laugh out loud.

So working indoors without the context of a Renaissance festival became a unique challenge, and we welcomed it. Penn & Teller flew to Minneapolis from their home in Fullerton, California, to work with us at the Comedy Cabaret a couple of times, staying at my house to save money.

Penn lived in the basement; Teller inhabited an upstairs bedroom. My young sons, Pat and Pete, were intrigued with our houseguests' unusual skills. Penn & Teller generously shared some of their best stuff with the boys.

Just as Pat was getting ready to take a shower, Teller appeared with a deck of cards, asked Pat to pick one out of the deck and not show it to him. Pat selected, say, the queen of hearts and placed it back in the deck. Teller smiled darkly and left. When Pat stepped out of the shower, the queen of hearts was plainly visible in the fog on the bathroom mirror.

Penn taught Pat how to play three-card Monte, the classic street game for suckers, illegal in many states. Some years later, Pat was in Las Vegas with some friends and set up a three-card Monte game on a side street. I got a phone call late that night; Pat was in the county jail. It took a couple of calls from Jules Smith, our festival friend and lawyer who seemed to know people everywhere, to spring him. Pat says to this day: Teller taught him some cool magic, and Penn taught him how to get arrested.

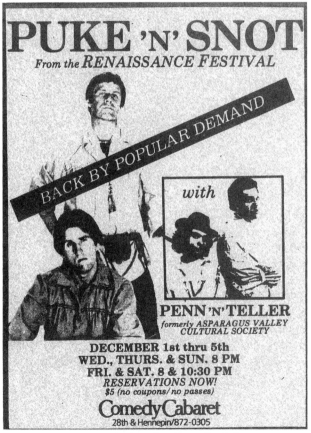

P & S & P & T at the Comedy Cabaret

In December of 1982 you could have bought a five-dollar ticket (no coupons/no passes) to watch Puke & Snot with Penn & Teller.

Penn thought himself a musician. He played bass, I played acoustic guitar, Teller had an electronic keyboard, and Joe played a mean tambourine. So we began and ended every show with a song we wrote specifically for that appearance, usually something from the Stones with new lyrics tailored to the evening.

One of these early shows at the Cabaret featured the debut of Mofo the Psychic Gorilla, the first public appearance of the disembodied simian head that was to become one of Penn & Teller's signature pieces in future shows. In the climactic mind-reading moment, I was onstage with a hand mirror; Joe was stationed at the door to the club with another hand mirror, and we positioned them so Mofo could "look" out the door and down the street where Penn was showing the playing card to an audience member. An inspired piece of lunacy, one of the funniest Penn & Teller bits we ever saw. We were proud and happy to be part of it.

Our fans followed us indoors. Scott Novotne and Stephanie Hodge, who ran the Comedy Cabaret, were looking for acts that went beyond standup, and they thought we were funny. We quickly realized that while bringing in Penn & Teller made for a great show, they were beginning to break out in Los Angeles, and would soon be too busy to play around with us. So we wrote our own opening half-hour, dug out some props, and the next time we showed up at the Comedy Cabaret it was Puke & Snot with Mark Sieve and Joe Kudla.

We wrote sketches we thought were funny; whether the audience thought so was immaterial. So Joe donned an Alpine hat, stuck a pipe in his teeth and became Wally Westheimer, the abused husband of then notorious sex therapist Ruth Westheimer.

Mark & Joe opening for Puke & Snot

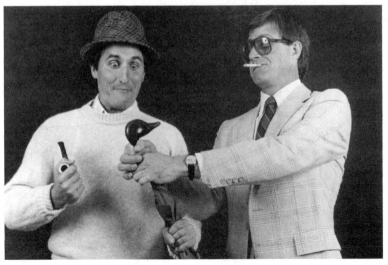

Joe is Wally Westheimer; I don't know who I am.

Precursors to Flight of the Conchords

We wrote parodies of classic sixties folk songs and appeared as Caleb and Dooley, crispy folksinger throwbacks harboring bitter memories of lost loves, but leading the audience in a sing-along celebrating each one. We did our version of Willie and Julio's "To All the Girls We've Loved Before" (*they weren't enough, we want some more...*).

A half-hour of this self-indulgent twaddle later, we reappeared as Puke & Snot in puffy shirts and jeans and did the self-indulgent twaddle we knew would actually work.

Working in Minneapolis at comedy clubs where we had a built-in audience was easy. They were very forgiving and allowed us to experiment without punishing us when we failed to be funny. When we showed up in other towns where no one knew us, however, things could get dicey.

An appearance at a NACA (National Association for Campus Activities) convention in Denver was a nightmare, one we referred to in subsequent years as the "reality check" show. A year before we had appeared in a comedy showcase at a regional NACA convention in San Jose. Everything clicked; the students loved the show, and we were the startled winners of a comedy showcase competition where the act with the most votes received an automatic twenty-two college booking in Arizona, California, and Utah.

Looking to build on that minor success, we traveled to Denver's NACA gathering to do our club material that featured interviews with the quirky characters that Joe created for the clubs in Minneapolis.

We bombed. The audience was actively antagonistic and had no clue what we were trying do. But we were committed, and an hour and a half later we were the most unpopular comedy duo ever to appear in Colorado. No one thought we were even remotely amusing. It was the stuff of legend. At least the Sons of Norway didn't throw things.

In the exhibit hall a few hours later, where all the agents and acts were set up at tables and booths to sell and book their shows, it was as if someone had posted a sign above our table: GET YOUR STDs HERE. No one stopped. In fact, people actually walked on the other side of the aisle to avoid eye contact with us. One college booking agent picked up some literature. He thought we might be a good fit for a show at the Colorado School of Mines. He took our card but never called.

Unappreciated in Denver, I was also finding classroom teaching more challenging than ever. I had developed motion sickness from my years on the education merry-go-round; I was weary of listening to my colleagues vent their frustrations in the teacher's lounge, and no longer interested in the hormone management that public secondary education had become.

One spring afternoon I inserted myself into a confrontation in the hall between the school nurse and two large transfer students. The nurse was in trouble, and I was the only other adult in sight. I ended up ducking punches and wrestling one of them to the marble floor. After filling out a police report and watching the kid taken away in a black-and-white, I walked into the teacher's lounge with my glasses broken and blood streaming from the bridge of my nose. Four teachers were playing cards at a table in the center of the room. An old faculty veteran looked up, shook his head and said, "I thought I told you to stay out of the halls between classes. It's dangerous out there."

I arrived home that day, growling and muttering. Jan, long-supporting and longer-suffering of my whiny dissertations on what was wrong with the education establishment, put down the pasta she was preparing for dinner, looked at me and said, "Why don't you quit?"

Startled, I responded, "Quit? Teaching? How would we pay the mortgage?"

I had never seriously considered it. I had been well-trained by my Depression-era parents to make sure the bird was firmly in the hand before beating the bushes with it.

Coolly and dispassionately, Jan explained that if my work was no longer satisfying, maybe I should consider finding a job I liked.

Puke & Snot was well-established, booking twenty-five week-ends a year, and we had just added the Sarasota Medieval Faire to our calendar. Jan's shop at the Minnesota festival was successful. Son Patrick had started a taxi service at the festival. He and his hockey teammates built two-wheelers in our backyard and were in business pulling and dragging customers all over the site. I was doing corporate video, commercials, and print modeling.

Jan said, "We'll find a way. But if you do this, you'd better make it pay."

Encouragement, accompanied by fair warning.

I spent that night and the next few days considering the possibilities. Agents had been asking if I was available. Directors had been willing to cast me. My wife was telling me to give it a shot.

Patrick and Peter working for Dad

A week later, I submitted my request for a leave of absence. Wouldn't want to dive in without a life preserver. Didn't have any idea how deep it might be. The leave option allowed me to scurry back to teaching if I found the wobbly world of an actor outside my financial comfort zone.

Joe had also found some interesting work. He did some priceless commercials, including a beer ad for a Minnesota brewer that played forever on local channels. He did hilarious video takeoffs of Dr. Frankenstein and Jacques Cousteau for corporate clients. We were cast together for a variety of projects, including a U.S. Military safety video. For years afterward people told us, "My son saw you in a training film when he was stationed in Korea."

The leave of absence was approved, and I got very busy very fast. I took every acting, modeling, and directing job that came my way. I did commercials for phone companies, beer companies, insurance companies, cable TV companies, shoe companies and car companies. I took a live ramp modeling job for a new line of Hanes underwear, and promised myself afterwards that I would pick my jobs more carefully. I worked onstage and off in every nook, alcove, niche, and cranny of the entertainment business.

Yogi Berra's famous advice to a young ballplayer echoed in my head: "When you come to a fork in the road, take it."

I did.

I have nothing to say.

12

LET'S KILL A GUY AND MAKE IT FUNNY

It proves what they always say: give the public what they want to see and they'll come out for it.
~ Red Skelton on the funeral of Harry Cohn

EARLIER IN 1982, Penn & Teller and I decided that Renaissance festivals needed a "big show," something owners could sell to the public that would guarantee colossal crowds of curious patrons every day. Festivals were full of one- and two-man variety acts, mimes, jugglers, musicians, and dancers. We were convinced a large cast of characters engaged in a big theatrical production would be an easy sell to festival producers.

So Penn & Teller returned to Minnesota to do some club shows with us and spend a couple of weeks at the house while we hammered out the details of what this show might be, who would perform it, who would buy it and how much money we could make writing, designing, casting and directing it.

The first step was to organize, so we became ACME Productions: Amazing Comical Magical Extravaganzas.

We charted our individual responsibilities for the pre-production period. Penn would be the official leader and take charge of publicity. Teller would design the show and create the props. I would write the script, direct the show and negotiate the contracts. Joe was to deal with the logistics and budget.

Next was to decide what the public wanted to see. We needed to create a scenario that would capture the imagination of the paying public in a way no current festival show had done. It needed to be dramatic, funny, and make use of the king, queen, and royal court, if possible, since they already had the costumes and attracted the most attention.

What we came up with, without the help of pharmaceuticals and thanks in no small part to Teller's macabre sense of humor and Penn's well-developed sense of the absurd, was a funny execution.

The result of ten-hour daily sessions for two weeks was *The Hanging of Mortimer Faust (he sold his pottery to the devil)*, wherein the aforesaid Mr. Faust was brought to trial by the Lord Mayor for practicing the black arts, namely, turning the mayor's wife into a duck.

Mr. Faust's defense: "Everybody knows she always WAS a duck."

Teller designed no less than twenty-two illusions, each triggered by one honk of Mr. Faust's duck call.

Honk! The mayor's pants came down.

Honk! The king's lunch came alive and walked off his plate.

Honk! A set piece collapsed!

It would happen once a day at noon. A man was tried before the court, found guilty of practicing "the black arts of witchcraft," and hung by his neck till he was dead.

Whee! We'd all pay to see that.

At the climax of the show, a rope would be strung around Faust's neck, a black hood placed over his head, and accompanied by a somber drum roll, he would drop through a trap door as the Lord Mayor announced to the crowd, "Thus endeth all who would profane the king's holiday by consorting with the devil!"

The curtain around the base of the scaffold would be removed, and a cry would go up: "He's gone!"

In the noose would be the victim's shirt, the crowd would hear a duck call, Faust would be standing on a wall fifty feet away. The final duck call would collapse the gallows with the Mayor on it, and Mortimer Faust would have his revenge.

It all sounded peachy, a comedy in one act complete with scantily clad women, wondrous magic effects, smoke and mayhem, horrid fantasy creatures, a gruesome killing, and absolutely no juggling or hammer dulcimer music. Festival owners were a competitive little group of egotists, they'd be clamoring to be the first to have this amazing, one-of-a-kind show. We were going to make millions!

From our original presentation materials:

THE HANGING OF MORTIMER FAUST *is a new outdoor magic show available to theme parks and Renaissance festivals beginning in spring 1983. It is a fast-paced, thrilling magical adventure in Renaissance style for the whole family. We bring to any Medieval or Renaissance festivities the color of a dozen rich and picturesque costumes; two towering set pieces, gilded, draped, and carved with comic gargoyles; spectacular magical vanishes, appearances, and transformations; sound, smoke, and flash effects by the country's outstanding film, stage, and circus technicians; a handsome and funny hero, a foiled villain, a gorgeous lady executioner, a jolly gravedigger, a dreadful monster, and a live duck.*

But more than a 25-minute outdoor extravaganza, we bring an event with unlimited promotional potential. Not only is every part of Mortimer Faust highly visual and photogenic, but each of the characters is a natural for media coverage and feature stories. We will be happy to help you devise and produce promotional plans and materials.

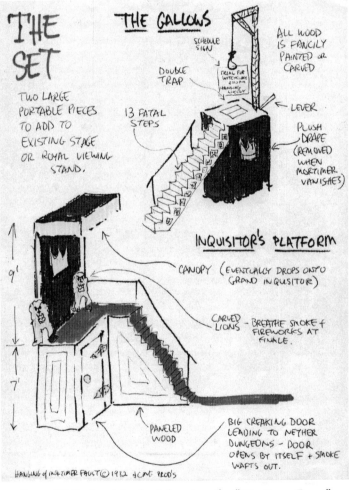

One of Teller's original set drawings for "Mortimer Faust"

The cast numbered thirteen, not including the festival royalty who would attend each show and become part of the action. The most complex character was the Dreaded Arachnid of Truth, a beautiful Muppet-like monster, half-human, half-spider, whose bite forced the victim to tell the truth and who Mortimer conquered with his duck call.

Set pieces, special effects, and costumes were to be built by friends of mine at Mixed Blood Theater. Penn & Teller had connections in the film and concert business, and Tom Berman (*Cat People, Invasion of the Body Snatchers, Halloween*, etc.) would build the Dreaded Arachnid. The Amazing Randi would design the actual "hanging," and we had Dar Robinson, the best stunt guy in Hollywood at the time, in reserve. (I had worked as a stunt actor at the wedding reception of Robinson's stunt designer a year before when he rigged a "hanging" of the bride and groom in an Old West theme village south of Minneapolis, so I knew he could safely execute actors).

Now, how to make this funny . . .

The Hanging of Mortimer Faust
"He sold his pottery to the devil."

ARRIVAL OF THE CHARACTERS. Music. Pomp. The ringing of bells.

As the royal court arrives, food and drink are served. The evil Inquisitor arrives with Mortimer Faust, well-guarded. We are about to witness a trial.

The Inquisitor charges Mortimer Faust with sorcery and accuses him of changing the Inquisitor's wife into a duck. Unfortunately, he confesses, the duck in question has already escaped custody. Always eager to help, Mortimer blows his magic duck call and the roast fowl upon which the king is dining is transformed into a live duck, dressed in hat, ribbons, and jewelry. The Inquisitor adoringly fusses over his wife.

The jolly gravedigger is interviewed as a witness for the prosecution when he comes to take Mortimer's measurements. Mortimer blows his duck call and the gravedigger's handkerchief changes color; his shovel rises in his hand and his pet skull (he carries it with him) starts chattering its teeth madly. He runs off, badly spooked, without giving a shred of useful testimony.

The Inquisitor calls in his scary lie-detector, a Muppet-like creature whose body is shrouded, but human. His head is a furry animated spider with glowing red eyes. He warns Mortimer that the bite of this creature compels the victim to confess. Dramatically, the creature, The Dreaded Arachnid of Truth, bites Mortimer, but it seems to have no more effect than a common mosquito bite. Blithely, Mortimer blows his duck call, the spider spins around and its rear lobe swells up, explodes, and drips green jelly.

Mortimer protests that the Inquisitor is incompetent. Assisted by his magic duck call, Mortimer accuses the Inquisitor of guzzling beer (whereupon beer in the Inquisitor's transparent mug vanishes); coming to court drunk (Inquisitor leans uncontrollably forward and sideways at weird and impossible angles like the Tin Man in the Wizard of Oz); behaving indecently (Inquisitor's pants drop); vandalizing state property (with a bang and a puff of smoke the canopy of the Inquisitor's platform drops on him); committing arson (smoke pours out from under the canopy).

The Inquisitor attempts to reply but finds his mouth full of ribbons. Mortimer: "Your majesty, I'm being accused by a duck-fornicating, drunken, exhibitionist vandal – a suicidal arsonist!"

The Inquisitor, having removed all the ribbons, states flatly that Mortimer, by his latest pranks, has proved himself a sorcerer beyond all doubt. He must be hanged. The royalty, who have taken quite a liking to Mortimer, reluctantly agree.

The Executioner makes a dramatic entrance, enhanced by her unexpected costume and the slapstick of slamming Mortimer behind the door to the nether regions. She collars Morty, puts a bag over his head, and amidst loud music marches him to the gallows. All the while, Mortimer seems blithely calm and happy. Intermittently, he blows his duck call, setting off little explosions in the pants of his guards.

The Executioner puts the noose around Mortimer's neck. The signal is given. Mortimer blows his duck call. The Executioner pulls the lever. Mortimer drops through the trap (out of sight within the draped base). The rope goes taut and sways ominously. The Executioner looks down into the trap and cries out. She raises the noose. It contains Mortimer's shirt, but no body. Guards pull away the drape of the gallows. Only the bare frame remains. Mortimer has vanished.

We hear the duck call from the balcony over the royalty's head. We see a veiled old lady we didn't notice before. She stands up, lifts her veil, removes her wig, and shows herself to be Mortimer himself—alive, well, and impudent as ever. He blows the duck call. The Inquisitor's pantaloons blow up like huge balloons.

Mortimer blows the duck call again. Smoke and flashes pour out of the mouths of the carved lions. He blows it one final time. There is a loud bang. A huge cloud of smoke envelopes him and, when it clears, he is gone.

The Inquisitor tries to set the guards in pursuit of Mortimer, but the king stops him, loudly declaring, "In my realm, a man hangs but once!"

The royalty dismisses the spectators with wishes for a merry day. And, to grand music, the happy court departs.

The script was to be as representative of the sensibilities of its creators as possible, which is to say, completely dismissive of any "Renaissance" language or atmosphere.

Inquisitor	*Your majesty, may I call forth the Dreaded Arachnid of Truth?*
King	*Yeah, bring out the weirdo with the bug.*

[AFTER MORTIMER HAS FIRMLY ESTABLISHED HIS MAGICAL CREDENTIALS]

Inquisitor:	*Well, I'll be a six-foot whale dick!*

[ALL THE ROYAL PAGES DO A GROUP DOUBLE TAKE AND RUN AWAY]

Inquisitor	*You are sentenced to die!*
Mortimer	*Good! How about placing me in a bag with a starving wolverine?*
Inquisitor	*No.*
Mortimer	*Okay, then how about injecting my ears with sausage and setting vultures on me? No? Then how about skinning me alive and rolling me in salt? Or paprika.*
Inquisitor	*No!*
Mortimer	*Okay then, your majesty, how about letting the Grand Inquisitor bore me to death?*
Inquisitor	*You will be hanged! Now!*
Mortimer	*No, wait, gouge out my eyes and poach eggs in the sockets.*

Inquisitor	*Enough!*
Mortimer	*Your majesty, I protest. The same man who thought of the Dreaded Arachnid of Truth, the man who has literally hundreds of interesting, nay, fascinating modes of killing people at his fingertips, proposes to do away with me in a simple hanging. How pedestrian!*
Inquisitor	*You will be hanged by the neck until dead!*
Mortimer	*How about till I'm tired? Till I'm ornery. Cranky? Ooh, I know, how about hang me by the neck till I'm sorry!*

Penn & Teller headed back to California. I sat down and made my list of festival owners who would pay anything to have this show. After putting together the costs of hiring actors, building sets, creating special effects and trucking the whole sideshow to festivals, I realized we might have a project whose costs exceeded the actual annual entertainment budget of most festivals. Undeterred by this ominous reality, I started calling people.

Owners loved the idea. The price, however, inspired a deafening silence at the other end of the line, then a throat-clearing "Okay, we'll talk it over and call you."

Only one owner wanted me to fly out and show him the details, our old friend The King in Houston. If anyone could mount this show successfully at his festival, it would be The King. So I put together a professional marketing packet complete with Teller's beautiful hand-drawn set and costume designs, bought a plane ticket and headed for Texas once again, determined to sell

The King a product that would make him the envy of every festival producer in the country.

I arrived on site on a beautiful, sunny day. I parked my rental car at the office, grabbed my sales packet and strolled in. The King was in his truck out on the site, so I walked out to look for him. Within minutes, he drove up, waved me into the passenger seat and said, "I want to show you some of the new stuff we're building here. Have a drink."

I looked down and in the console between the seats was a quart of Jim Beam, two glasses and a bucket of ice. It was ten in the morning. He poured two large drinks as he drove, pointing out the highlights of the tour and handing me my morning bracer.

I pretended to sip mine and wondered what in God's name I was thinking, coming back to this place where normal human interaction was defined this way. Whenever we'd step out of the truck to examine a new stage area or shop, I dumped part of my drink on the ground. In ten minutes, we were back at his office. He sat back in his desk chair and said, "Now what's this big show you want me to buy?"

I launched into the pitch, beginning with the entertainment principles behind "the big show," why it would work at any festival, the obvious promotional possibilities of a picture in the Friday Houston paper of a man about to be killed on Saturday for the entertainment of the general public, how we thought that fit perfectly into the local cultural mix and the way Texans generally felt about capital punishment, and on and on.

He listened for three minutes, and then held up his hand. "Whoa. I know what the concept is. I get it. It sounds good. Just tell me what it's going to cost."

"Twenty-five thousand for seven weekends."

"I'll give you ten thousand for two weekends."

"Okay, I'll take it back to the boys and let you know."

"By the way, you and Snot interested in coming back this fall?"

"Not unless you've found the money you owe us from last season."

"Bobby's still got your money; I told you that."

"Then we're not interested."

"Fair enough."

I was back on the plane that afternoon, and after a brief conversation with the other principals at the World Headquarters of ACME Productions in Fullerton, it was determined by voice vote that the cost of mounting the show would far exceed the ten grand The King would pay for two weeks. And since *The Hanging of Mortimer Faust* seemed to be an idea that was far ahead of its time, even though its time was four hundred years in the past, it would go on the shelf only to be revived if it became clear that there were owners and producers out there who had the balls and the bank account to stage it.

It's still in the filing cabinet in my basement office.

13

BILLY AND ME

*The kid doesn't chew tobacco, smoke, drink,
curse, or chase broads. I don't see how
he can possibly make it.*
~ Richie Ashburn

MAKING THE VARSITY BASEBALL team at St.
John's the spring of 1961 pretty much guaranteed that I wouldn't
open a book for the rest of the school year. By early June I was firmly
established as a dependable starting pitcher and, at the same time
with little or no effort compiled a dismal grade-point average and
was placed on academic probation.

I underwent a humiliating visit to the dean in the company
of my concerned parents. Much was made of the cost incurred and
the time wasted and how if had I been a typical student, I would
have been let go. But the dean, happily for me, was Father Dunstan
Tucker, the legendary former baseball coach. He'd seen me play and
wanted me around the next spring. So I was given a reprieve, told I
needed to maintain a B-average the next semester or be dismissed.
I gratefully determined to follow Easy Ed's dictate to work hard to
avoid the cellar and find a place in the comfortable middle.

The following year we had a losing record in another typically weather-shortened Minnesota small-college season. I was a staff veteran by now, a sophomore who felt I should win every time I went out there; but I ended the spring 0-4, even though I ranked high in the league in strikeouts and ERA.

That summer I saw a notice in the Minneapolis paper for a tryout camp at Metropolitan Stadium, home of the Minnesota Twins. Three days of practice and games, open to anyone; give it your best shot and you could end up with a professional contract. I headed to Bloomington, Minnesota, to do just that.

More than three hundred big league hopefuls dotted the field as I walked out onto the impossibly green grass of Metropolitan Stadium that first sunny day in early June. Some of them were obviously just there for the experience; others were dead serious about this chance to follow their dream.

I stood in line at the bullpen in right field watching other pitching candidates throw for their allotted five minutes. I noticed that whenever anyone threw hard, the scouts with the clipboards paid close attention and occasionally wrote something down.

Whenever a pitcher started throwing junk, curve balls or knuckle balls, they dropped the clipboards to their sides and chatted with each other about lunch or girlfriends. I resolved that when they handed me the ball, I would try to knock the catcher down with fastballs, more fast balls, and nothing but fast balls.

Finally, the front of the line. The guy ahead of me was throwing spinners in the dirt and the scouts were falling asleep. Somebody tossed me a new ball and said, "You're up."

I stepped onto the perfectly groomed bullpen mound and the catcher squatted behind the plate. We were enclosed in a tight green envelope of protective fence that made it seem like I was about to start throwing in a small room. I felt like I was right on top of the plate. I was pumping adrenaline so fast I took only five pitches to warm up.

I threw hard and harder. Nothing but strikes. Out of the corner of my eye I saw the scouts watching carefully and making notes. At the end of the session, the catcher took off his mitt and checked his hand. I remembered Tommy Bofenkamp and I smiled.

I made the cut for day two, and again for day three. The final session was dedicated to an all-day game where each remaining pitcher got one inning. I did well, shutting down four batters on one infield hit and a couple of strikeouts.

Sitting in the stands behind the third-base dugout at the end of a ten-hour game, we looked around and tried to figure out the odds. Would anybody's name be called? Would we all get sent home? Was there anybody here good enough to play professional ball?

A large guy with a clipboard came up the steps from the field and called for quiet. "The following players take your gear and come with me: number two, number six, number fourteen, number twenty-three, number twenty-nine, and number thirty-three. The rest of you, the Twins organization thanks you very much; you can go home."

A tiny tremor went up my spine and raised the hair on the back of my neck. The numbers were on our backs, I was pretty sure mine was thirty-three. Somebody clapped me on the shoulder and congratulated me. Six of us made the cut, and I was one of them.

As nonchalantly as I could, I grabbed my bag and glove and joined the little group of sweaty, happy ballplayers as we followed the paunchy guy with the clipboard into the bowels of the stadium, past other paunchy guys with clipboards and cigars, into what looked like a boardroom with a giant mahogany table and a dozen red upholstered chairs. Nobody was talking.

"Wait here," the beefy guy said. He closed the door behind him and we were alone, six excited young guys with absolutely no idea what was supposed to happen next.

In a few minutes, the door opened and somebody's name was called. He got up, waved and left. Ten minutes later, again, the door opened, another name called, another player gone. This went on for an hour, until I was alone in the boardroom. I sat there for what seemed like another hour and became convinced they forgot I was there. I looked for another way out, a way to quietly escape and avoid the humiliation of walking past whoever was out there.

Suddenly the door opened and a very familiar, very friendly face walked in, another guy holding a clipboard, but one I recognized instantly. "Hi," he said, "I'm Billy Martin."

"Yeah, I know," I blurted. I was face to face with an MVP, an all-star second baseman for the Yankees. He played his final game the year before with the Twins and was now a scout in their system. I hadn't seen him anywhere on the field or in the stands during the three days during the tryouts. But here he was, talking to me.

He got right to the point. "They want me to get your name on this contract, but I think I should tell you it's not a very good one. It's a one-year Class C contract for five hundred dollars a month, no bonus. Without a bonus, they don't have nothin' invested; they might watch you for two weeks in Orlando and, if you don't impress 'em, they'll cut you, and you lose your college eligibility. Then there's the military draft to think about. All I'm saying is you've got a good arm and with another year or two of college you should be able to get some bonus money. It's up to you. But I'd talk to mom and dad first, maybe a lawyer."

I probably would've signed the contract on the spot if he told me to. I was pretty sure the guys who sent him in to talk to me wouldn't have approved of his forthright description of their offer, but I was grateful. He was definitely on the player's side. Here he was, an MVP, a former Yankee and world-class ballplayer, quietly helping a young farm kid from Long Prairie make a very important decision.

I took the contract and thanked him. We walked out into the office where George Brophy, the head of the Twins minor league operation was sitting at his desk.

Brophy: "Well, kid, you gonna join the Twins?"

Martin: "He's gonna take it home and talk to his parents, right?"

I nodded.

Brophy frowned and glanced down at my stat sheet from St. John's.

"0-4 this spring? Why are we looking at you again?"

Martin chimed in, "No sticks, George," a reference to my college teammates' lack of hitting support during my starts that spring.

Brophy looked disappointed. "Well, come back soon; we'll give you and your folks some tickets behind home plate; we'd like to have you play some ball for us."

I thanked him; Martin winked and I was gone.

When I got home my family was proud and excited, and when we talked about it, we all agreed that Billy was probably right. Ben and Helen were practical, down-to-earth people who wanted me in college until I had the degree that neither of them had the opportunity to get. Finishing college seemed like the right thing to do. If I was good enough to play pro ball I'd be good enough in two years.

A few weeks later Mom and Dad and their oldest kid all drove in the big white Buick LeSabre to Bloomington, picked up our tickets, sat behind home plate in the same ballpark I'd played in just weeks earlier and watched the Twins win. I told Mr. Brophy after the game that thanks anyway; I'd be heading back to St. John's for my junior year.

Brophy shifted his cigar and said, "We'll be keeping an eye on you."

14

PROMOTING THE BRAND

The festival business is a cruel and shallow money trench, a long plastic highway where thieves and pimps run free and good men die like dogs. There's also a negative side.

~ Me

OKAY, THAT'S NOT MY QUOTE. I stole that line from Hunter Thompson who was talking about the television business. It's all right; stealing good material is how many Renaissance festival acts stay fresh.

From the beginning Puke & Snot was subversive. Almost anti-Renaissance. We injected anachronisms into the show at every opportunity. The contrast between the period-specific Renaissance performer who took his costuming seriously and always spoke "the speech I pray you trippingly on the tongue" – and what we wanted Puke & Snot to be – couldn't have been clearer.

Dropping character while in costume, while anathema to most entertainment directors, was exactly what we thought should happen. So Joe's, "It was the best of times, it was the worst of times…" was followed by my "…details at eleven!"

Mark Antony's, "Friends, Romans, countrymen, lend me your ears..." was tagged with my, "He wants to make a necklace out of them."

Joe loudly declaimed, "I come not to bury Caesar but to praise him!" and my response from the audience was, "It's about time you showed up."

It was Python-esque, and, we thought, terribly droll.

We had good friends on the festival circuit who were infamous for never dropping character. They were unfailingly infuriating. The reigning champ was David Casey, an original member of the best whip, dagger, and juggling show that ever graced a stage, *Rogue, Oaf and Fool.*

David's "Fool" was a balding, spindle-legged grinning piece of Renaissance perfection who never broke character when he wore that costume. Even backstage. I'd see him before a performance and ask him if he wanted to play golf the following week.

He was a fanatical golfer. What I got was a gap-toothed smile, a puzzled look, and the question: "Golf? What is this that you speak of, kind sir? I know not of this 'golf.'"

Most actors hanging out between shows never worried about staying in character; it was something you stepped into like a costume just before you walked onstage. David was Fool ten hours a day, non-stop. If I wanted to speak with David, I had to wait until the closing cannon when Fool got into David's street clothes. It was certainly artsy, and David was a brilliant improv actor who ended up working with the Big Apple Circus in New York. But it was definitely irritating. Joe and I were never in character. More accurately, we were always exactly who we were.

The most sensuous word in the English language

Ron Boulden, an old friend who ran the entertainment at Scarborough Faire in Dallas, once called me about doing a season at his festival. Ron said, "I want you guys to be the leaders down here; I want you to show the younger actors how it's done."

I said, "Ron, do you know what we do? We make fun of the whole idea—you really don't want us leading anything. We'd destroy the whole idea of community you're trying to foster. We're hired guns; just bring us in and we'll make people laugh and get out of town before anybody realizes we're not that funny."

We weren't offered a contract.

But we were getting requests from other festivals to produce a Puke & Snot show, even if we weren't available to do it. I wrote a script and directed two young college actors at Disney World one summer in a Puke & Snot takeoff I called *Redgrave and Scroup*.

It was very successful in six weeks of performances, and Disney asked about installing the show permanently outside the Italian pavilion at EPCOT. We had demonstrated that with the right actors, the show worked. So it was probably inevitable that we'd eventually start hiring other actors, training them and sending them out around the country.

The first clones appeared at the Kansas City festival in the early eighties, and immediately became the most popular show on site. Bruce Bohne played Puke, and later went on to a successful stage and film career, spending many seasons at the Guthrie Theater in Minneapolis and playing Marge's deputy in the Coen Brother's hit movie *Fargo*. Dean Hanus played Snot, and actually worked with me our first season in Colorado when Joe wasn't available; he was doing a run at Chanhassen Dinner Theater in Minneapolis in a production of *Dial M for Murder*.

The next duo went to Maryland, Jim Doughan and Geoff Ewing. Jim became a major player at Dudley Riggs' Brave New Workshop, then headed for Los Angeles and worked with The Groundlings. Jim has since appeared in dozens of movies and television series. Geoff ended up in New York where he produced and starred in an award-winning off-Broadway play about Muhammad Ali.

Geoff Ewing and me in "Lemons" at Mixed Blood

Joe Keyes and GregAlan Williams were our next team; they performed in Maryland for one season. Joe came back and admitted he'd become a "laugh junkie" and started writing and performing stand-up comedy, ending up in Los Angeles writing for the *Roseanne* show and doing club work. Greg found success as an actor, writer, and speaker. He became a regular on *Baywatch* and had recurring roles on *The West Wing* and *The Sopranos*. He won an Emmy as a high school basketball coach in the television movie *Fast Break to Glory*, and he became a real-life action hero in 1992 when he saved the life of a Japanese-American man by pulling him to safety during the Los Angeles riots. He wrote a book about this experience, *A Gathering of Heroes: Reflections on Rage and Responsibilities: A Personal Memoir of the Los Angeles Riots.*

Michael Levin and Peter Simmons were yet another team we sent to Maryland, and with the down time they had between weekends they came up with a very funny movie script they called *Pyook and Snotte: The Filme.* The beautifully crafted yarn featured pirates, treachery in the English court, the kidnapping of a Queen, mistaken identities, and elaborate slapstick fights and chases.

I asked Joe Camp, the producer of the popular "Benji" movies to look at the script. He estimated the production costs for both Minnesota and Los Angeles and said he'd love to work on it, but he was in the middle of another doggie masterpiece and it would have to wait.

I ended up getting a cast together around some microphones in a studio in Minneapolis and produced it as a one-hour comedy CD. Cecil Allen, an Irish actor and producer and an old friend from our theater days in Minneapolis recorded the narrator role in a Dublin studio. It was the second CD in our collection: "Puke & Snot's Comical Bum."

Many of our friends and fellow actors who used the Puke & Snot show as a launching pad for their careers still refuse to put the show on their resumes, a decision that demonstrates an admirable instinct for self-preservation.

While our clones were spreading the Puke & Snot gospel, Joe and I booked any and all festivals we could con into a contract—festivals in Arizona, Miami, San Diego, and Toronto. Some of them were one-or two-week adventures run by promoters who thought it might be a quick score but ended up losing their life savings.

One festival in particular was memorable, if only for the lessons it could teach potential entrepreneurs whose business acumen wasn't as finely tuned as it needed to be to keep them from bankruptcy court. We got a call from a real estate developer in San Diego asking us to sign a contract for a three-week festival he was planning in Balboa Park. We had done this festival the previous summer under different management, but he apparently bought the show and wanted to expand. He had Penn & Teller committed and wanted Puke & Snot.

San Diego had beaches, golf courses, professional baseball, everything we needed to rationalize a three-week show where every cent we made would no doubt be spent before we returned home. We said yes. But having already done the San Diego show, we had a few contractual requirements. Our daily performance schedule needed to start at eleven A.M., take a three-hour break, and resume at two P.M. with three more shows before closing at six P.M. Unbelievably, they agreed.

So on the opening Saturday, we stepped out on the stage of the Organ Pavilion at Balboa Park and dazzled the onlookers with our well-honed shtick. After the show, we strolled backstage, thence to the parking lot where our trusty rental car was parked, and drove to Mission Beach, ten minutes away, changing in the car into swimsuits.

We rented a couple of boogie boards, dove into the surf and emerged an hour later, wrinkled and happy. It took another half-hour to change, grab a couple of tacos and get back to the Organ Pavilion, where we parked the car and ran out onstage for our two o'clock show. We followed this routine each day for three weekends and as far as we knew, no one but Penn & Teller was aware of it.

This was a fine gig, until we realized our real estate developer was bouncing checks. We discovered that the "actor" who had played Lord Mayor the previous summer wanted to repeat his role, but the new owner had turned him down. The Lord Mayor, a prominent San Diego lawyer, was not to be trifled with. He pulled some strings at City Hall and when the owner showed up to pick up his liquor license for the festival, the clerk said, "What liquor license?"

The lawyer ended up with the beer and wine concessions and the owner ended up with bills he couldn't pay, including the salaries of some of the actors. Joe and I got to the bank early on Monday after the first weekend and our checks were cashed. Penn & Teller's checks weren't, and Penn went ballistic on the poor man.

Me, Jan, Joe and friend Nancy in Sarasota

By the end of the festival, the lawyer had no money and took to hiding in his seaside home and not answering his phone. We later heard that Penn & Teller showed up daily at his house, pounding on the door and yelling at him to sell his boat and car and pay them. He put up with that for a few days and eventually opened the door and gave them their money.

I still have the bounced checks as souvenirs of our happy days in San Diego.

Besides sending out actors to spread the Puke & Snot name to the four corners of the earth, we decided sometime in the early eighties to launch our own line of clothing, giving our fans a chance to make their own fashion statements. We asked Wayne Walstead, a sometime festival performer and top-notch graphic designer, to come up with a tee-shirt design that would inspire the average patron to part with a few bucks in the name of festival chic.

Wayne's first shirt design for P & S

TENTH ANNIVERSARY END OF THE WORLD TOUR

More of Wayne's world

Festival owners weren't inclined to let entertainers to go into business; in fact they didn't allow it. Those of us who were building a following saw our crowds as a marketing opportunity to fight for; so in keeping with our subversive roots, we decided to make the first festival tee shirt available to the public in the fall of 1983.

Wayne's first design effort built on our own attempts to take the show around the country. It was the first of several "world tour" designs that became big sellers.

The festival gave us a firm "No" when we asked if we could open a shop near our stage. So Joe took the first batch of shirts, stuffed them in burlap bags, stood under a tree after our shows and sold them like the contraband they were. People snapped them up. We sold out our first printing in two weekends.

Some long-time festival performers with a more purist approach than ours often said that Puke & Snot were responsible for cheapening and commercializing the Renaissance concept. I think they're partly correct, but we were too humble to take full credit.

The owners who allowed craftsmen to sell plastic lampshades and "made in China" pottery got there first. Our tee shirts, caps, sweatshirts, CDs, and the thousand other Puke & Snot bric-a-brac that was sold and collected over the years were mostly made, by hand, in my basement, by Joe and me.

We were often there all-night long, like a couple of crazed Santa's elves, preparing the next day's merchandise, making each shirt on handmade looms Joe built in his backyard with tools he constructed from my original designs.

Those were the days. I don't know how we found time to rehearse. Nowadays, of course, having happily joined the global marketplace, everything we sell is made in a sweatshop in Bangalore.

15

THE NEXT LEVEL

People think we make $3 million and $4 million a year.
They don't realize that most of us only make $500,000.
~ Pete Incaviglia

MY JUNIOR YEAR IN COLLEGE spun by quickly, affected only minimally by the creeping onset of an awareness that the world outside our little protective cocoon of learning in the forests of Central Minnesota was getting more dangerous and more complicated. The country's growing involvement in Vietnam included the attendant threat to those of us of draft age to become part of that action, whether or not we thought it was moral or right. The news of the assassination of JFK, the beginnings of the civil rights movement, and the awakening of the counter-culture pointed to a shifting of the national consciousness and an unsettling of the miniature world where we lived and studied with the monks of St. Benedict. We kept our heads down, went to mass regularly and spent as much time in the gym as we could justify away from the books.

After the spring baseball season I was now firmly established as one of the two aces of the pitching staff. The other was my good friend Bob Johnson from Nisswa, Minnesota, a shy kid with the best curve ball any of us had ever seen.

I was asked by a scout in the Dodger organization if I wanted to play semi-pro ball that summer. He told me he'd recommend me to Rapid City of the Basin League in South Dakota, a "semi-professional" league sponsored by the NCAA and created years before for serious college ballplayers to compete at a high level without losing their college eligibility.

I had heard about the Basin League and some of the big names in major league ball who had played there. The chance to spend a summer finding out how I measured up against players from all over the country was too good to pass up; so in early June I found myself throwing on the sidelines at Fitzgerald Stadium, home of the Rapid City Chiefs. I was surrounded by major college thoroughbreds, the kind of guys who carried their newspaper clippings with them on the front seats of their cars.

"Hey, Frog."

I turned around to see one of my childhood buddies from Ellsworth, Jerry Matthieson, the best switch hitting all-around athlete our tiny burg had ever produced. He was playing catch right behind me. I hadn't seen him since I'd left town seven years earlier. He had driven from Minnesota to try out, even though he wasn't in college and knew this was a college league. He stepped into the box and began knocking balls all over the park. Yeah, good old Ellsworth was well represented.

After a week of practice, it was clear to all of us pitchers that there were only a few spots available in the rotation. The Rapid City Chiefs had sought out some of the best arms in the country, from the Big Ten, the SEC, and Division I colleges all over the nation.

We had four all-Americans who were locks, and ten more of us competed for the final three spots. It was just a matter of time before we were headed home. We each met with the Topps bubble gum representative. Some of us took the one hundred dollars offered for the rights to our baseball card if we ever made the big leagues; most of us turned him down. We were warned that if anyone asked if we were being paid, we were to say we had jobs coaching little league teams or working construction. If we made the team, it was understood that somehow, somewhere, three hundred dollars per month would be ours.

The day the final cut was to be announced, word came to us that a new league was being formed in Illinois, and that those of us who were cut in Rapid City would be flown there to help form the six teams that would make up the new semi-pro league modeled after the successful Basin League. Those who wanted to join another league in Canada would be flown there.

Two days later, I was on my first plane ride, on my way to Illinois, feeling very much a professional. Even though my talents weren't fully appreciated in South Dakota, I was apparently good enough for the Dodgers to invest in a plane ticket.

Tryouts in Lincoln, Illinois, went on for three days, each of us getting a chance to show what we could do. All the players were assembled in Lincoln to be assigned to one of the six teams in the brand-new Central Illinois Collegiate League. I threw as hard as I could for as long as I could, having already learned that a heavy fastball got attention faster than a dinky curve or a lazy knuckleball.

A few days into the process, two black college players from a school I'd never heard of returned one night to the dorm and told us they had to go home. They couldn't buy gas or groceries or get served in any restaurants in Lincoln, and they'd been threatened more than once. They were very afraid and needed to get out of town.

I thought at the time that – here we all were in Lincoln, the Illinois town named after the president who wrote the Emancipation Proclamation, a statue of him in the public park – and these two college kids can't even buy gas for their car. This can't be right.

We all tried to get them to stay, but no one could assure them things would be any better if they did. They were gone the next morning, and nothing was said about it thereafter. It was as if they had never existed.

It was 1963; civil rights was not even a passing concern for the vast majority of us white college boys. Most of us were blissfully unaware that black ballplayers might be having problems none of us ever experienced. In fact, the photo of the six teams that lined up on opening day of the first summer of the CICL's existence hardly looks like a cross section of America at that time.

We played a round robin of three games that day. Tickets were free to the public as the league proudly launched itself to its Illinois market. Bloomington, Galesburg, Champagne-Urbana, Springfield, Peoria, and Lincoln were the chosen cities. At some point during our first game that day, our manager Jack Horenberger called everyone together in the dugout to introduce an ancient gentleman who ambled over from the stands to say hello. He walked with a cane, had a big cigar stuffed in his teeth and looked to be in his eighties.

CENTRAL ILLINOIS COLLEGIATE BASEBALL LEAGUE

"Baseball Jamboree" Springfield, Illinois on Saturday. July 27, 1963.

TEAMS

Bloomington	Lincoln
Champaign-Urbana	Peoria
Galesburg	Springfield

Ten of these guys ended up in the Bigs.

The coach said, "Boys, I want you to meet Mr. Branch Rickey. He just stopped by today to wish us well."

We all said hi to the old gent. He sat down and watched the rest of the inning with us before walking stiffly back to his seat in the stands. I was aware at the time that he was an important figure in major league baseball, but it wasn't until later that I found out what Mr. Branch Rickey meant to baseball and why our manager seemed so much in awe of him that day. This was the innovative major league baseball executive who broke baseball's color barrier by signing Jackie Robinson and later drafting the first Hispanic superstar Roberto Clemente. He created the framework for the modern minor-league farm system. Other than Jack Horenberger, I'm not sure anyone else in that dugout that day knew anything about him.

I was assigned to the Bloomington Bobcats, and I called home excitedly to report that I made the club and would be spending the rest of the summer playing ball in Illinois. I was a "professional," even though my checks would technically be coming from a part-time job.

NCAA rules prevented us from actually being paid to play, so a system was set up, similar to the Basin League, where all of us were to be assigned jobs in the community, many of them simple make-work jobs provided by baseball-friendly businesses. I would be cutting grass and doing maintenance at a housing project.

Most days there was nothing to do, I'd bring a book and sit in the shade reading for a few hours, then head to practice or a game. We played seven games a week, double headers on Saturdays with Mondays off. The competition was the best I'd ever seen.

At St. John's I'd been able to get my fastball past most hitters without worrying about the location. Here I found many hitters could see it coming and had no problem pounding it if it wasn't on the corners or the knees. I knew I needed another pitch, so I learned to throw a slider in a week.

It was a dream summer. Every pitcher got his innings and threw in relief when necessary. My first start came at a game in Galesburg, I was so pumped up I struck out nine and walked six in six innings, I got the win when our shortstop, Doug Rader, hit one out with a man on to put us ahead in the sixth (Doug was one of the stars of the league that summer, and enjoyed a long career as a player and manager in the bigs).

I went on to win my first three starts, posting a decent 2.13 ERA for the summer and getting my share of strikeouts.

I had proved one thing to myself: I could compete at the next level. I was determined to go back to St. John's for the best spring of my life and dominate the MIAC Conference. Billy Martin was right. I was going after that signing bonus and pay off my college loans.

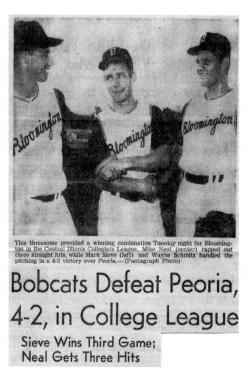

This threesome provided a winning combination Tuesday night for Bloomington in the Central Illinois Collegiate League. Mike Neal (center) rapped out three straight hits, while Mark Sieve (left) and Wayne Schmitz handled the pitching in a 4-2 victory over Peoria.— (Pantagraph Photo)

Bobcats Defeat Peoria, 4-2, in College League

Sieve Wins Third Game; Neal Gets Three Hits

Me on the left, playing in Peoria

16

LOST BALLS

Although golf was originally restricted to wealthy,
overweight Protestants, today it's open to
anyone who owns hideous clothing.
~ Dave Barry

PLAYING GOLF DURING THE WEEK was a definite perk in the weekend performer's lifestyle, one that Joe and I valued greatly. Courses usually aren't crowded, often just a few doctors and lawyers cluttering up the tee boxes. Clearly an opportunity to play good courses at non-weekend rates, and we took advantage of it whenever possible.

I was standing on a bench passing the hat after a show at the Kansas City festival in '87 when a guy in a baseball cap and sunglasses dropped a five dollar bill in the cup and asked me how long I'd been doing the show. I recognized him immediately as Tom Watson, one of the best professional golfers in the world, someone Joe and I had watched for years. He and his wife and their two children had just seen our show and had apparently enjoyed it. We chatted for awhile and Mr. Watson stunned me by inviting me to a round of golf at his club the following Friday and dinner at his house afterwards. He asked me if Joe played. I paused.

Joe was a local club-throwing legend on the municipal courses of the Twin Cities. Everyone had stories about his volatile relationship with the game of golf. My oft repeated question to Joe on the golf course, usually after he had sent another golf club sailing into the pond after a bad shot, was: "You really don't like this game very much, do you...?"

But he did. He played it with all the fatalistic fervor of an addict, knowing his game was probably not going to get much better, but absolutely tenacious in trying to solve the mysteries of the weight shift. Once we were playing at a lovely mountain course in Colorado, I hit my drive into the woods and said, "Good grief, what a horrible shot." Or words to that effect.

Joe stalked past me, stuck a tee in the ground and said darkly, "Oh yeah? Just watch *this*."

So yes, when Mr. Watson asked me if Joe played, I paused. I had a momentary vision of Joe throwing his driver and fracturing Tom Watson's skull. It would be difficult to explain to his wife and children. But I said, "Yes, he loves the game."

"Good!" he replied. "We'll see you next weekend."

The Watsons left and I casually asked Joe if he'd like to play golf next Friday.

He said "Maybe. Where?"

"Here in Kansas City. With Tom Watson."

"With...? Give me a minute; I have to think about it. *Yes!*"

I told him that if he did his Incredible Hulk routine during this particular *very special* upcoming round of golf, when we got to the parking lot I'd take my putter and bend it around his neck. He promised to be good.

The following Friday we followed Mr. Watson's directions from the KC airport to the Hallbrook Country Club in South Kansas

City. We joined him and Jeff, the assistant pro. Joe and Tom teamed up against Jeff and me for a few dollars to make it interesting. As if it wasn't already interesting enough: playing a round of golf from the tips on a difficult course with a guy who had five British Open trophy replicas on his office bookshelf.

We teed off on the first hole, a long par four that I bogeyed, and Watson, incredibly, triple bogeyed. I remember thinking, "I can stay with this guy."

That was the last bad hole he had that day, I had many to look forward to. Seventeen holes later, I staggered into the clubhouse with the distinct impression that this was the hardest course I had ever played in my life. Watson shot a 77. Jeff the pro recorded an 82. Joe and I flailed away and didn't get close to breaking 90.

That round of golf was memorable for many reasons, not the least of which was an occurrence on the fourth fairway. After a few holes of watching Joe attack the ball with his usual ferocity, Tom walked over to him on the fairway, stood behind him and tried to get Joe to loosen his shoulders to free up his swing.

Joe stood there for a long moment with The International Legend of Golf directly behind him correctly aligning his shoulders. He looked at me warily and said: "What exactly is he doing back there?"

He then stepped up to his ball and hit it into a swamp.

Watson shrugged and said, "Funny game, golf."

Much later, after an excellent meal, many laughs, and more bourbon than your average pirate crew would swill in a week, we got our final swing lesson as we stood in Watson's garage at midnight. It had something to do with an athletic stance and bending the knees. It's foggy now; but I remember it all making sense at the time.

Relaxing with our golf instructor

The following summer I got a phone call from Tom's wife Linda; she asked us if we could come to Kansas City for a surprise performance at Tom's fortieth birthday party. Since it would take place on a Saturday in September, and we were already committed to the Minnesota festival, I told her we probably couldn't make it.

A few days later, Tom called and asked about our schedule. "Is there an airport near the Minnesota festival?"

"Yeah, Flying Cloud is about eight miles."

"If I had a plane waiting for you, could you fly in after your last show on Saturday?"

"Possibly."

"You could land at the downtown KC airport. I'll have a car meet you; you'll be at the house before the party gets started. You can do a show by the pool, we'll get you back to the airport early the next morning and you won't miss a thing at the festival."

"Okay, but you're going to regret it."

September 1st rolled around, a hot Saturday at the festival. We got permission to blow off our five P.M. show so we'd have enough time to make this gig happen.

At 4:15 we pulled up to Flying Cloud; a small plane was waiting. We boarded, still in costume and sweating profusely. The pilot had a cooler of beer ready, and we took off for a strange and well-oiled adventure in Missouri.

True to his word, Mr. Watson had a limo waiting for us when we landed. A quick trip through town and we arrived around six P.M., greeted at the front door by the Man himself. We were shown an upstairs bedroom where we changed clothes and emerged incognito, introduced to the guests as a couple of club pros from Minneapolis, friends of Tom's from college. Joe became Scotty McCracken and I was Chip Putnam.

To Joe's credit, he kept the Scottish accent throughout the evening, lending more credibility to his new identity as a professional golfer. Tom introduced us to his brother-in-law who was busily pouring drinks at the bar in the living room. Chuck was Linda's brother, a large, darkly funny presence whose sense of humor ran to the edgy. "Here you go, enjoy," he said as he handed us a couple of beers, "Everybody's out by the pool. You can join the Jews near the deep end or the Wasps at the shallow end."

I looked at Joe; I had no idea what Chuck was talking about. But as we strolled out to the pool, there were two large groups of people at either end of the pool – Linda's family and Tom's. Joe looked around and said, "All this party needs is Richard Dawson." But within an hour, as Chuck continued to pour and distribute quality beverages, everyone blended into one large happy celebration.

As the evening proceeded, Joe and I ended up in the amusement room shooting pool with the guests. We fielded many questions about how we knew Tom and managed to keep it vague enough to keep our covers from being blown. I gave some swing tips to a guy who wanted to tap my "professional" knowledge.

At ten P.M. two large buses arrived at the front driveway and everybody loaded onto them to head for a mini-golf tournament Tom and Linda had arranged. We were all divided into foursomes and played eighteen holes at a local putt-putt course where the prizes for winning were Waterford crystal (a lovely touch), and headed back to the house for the opening of the gifts and the lighting of the birthday candles.

Tom presented us with a couple of signature putters and some golf balls inscribed with "TOM'S FORE-TEE-ETH." Joe and I headed upstairs to change into tights and puffy shirts.

At a signal from Tom we stepped out to the pool where the guests were having their fore-tee-eth nightcap. He announced, "Ladies and gentlemen, your entertainment for the evening, Puke & Snot. You've been had."

It was the strangest, most surreal show we'd ever done. Nobody seemed able to grasp what these two golf pros were doing dressed as Renaissance rogues with swords and vegetables. We got some laughs and avoided falling into the pool during the sword fights. We changed clothes and piled into Chuck's SUV and he took us on a wild ride to our hotel, where we thankfully crashed. A quick four hours later, we were on the same plane heading back to Flying Cloud airport and the longest day of festival shows we'd ever done.

Tom and his family remain good friends and they always show up when Puke and Snot perform near Kansas City. Tom and I have a shared interest in politics and world events, and we continue to share a feisty correspondence about our favorite subjects.

I remind him that I'm the comedy expert and he's the golf pro. I tell him what's funny and he tells me that a mulligan is actually "lying three."

When Tom heard that Joe died, he said, "He made me laugh just by looking at him, and for that I'm forever grateful."

17

IT ONLY HURTS WHEN
I LAUGH

In certain trying circumstances, urgent circumstances, desperate circumstances, profanity furnishes a relief denied often to prayer.
~ Mark Twain

MY SENIOR YEAR at St. John's was a total commitment to whipping myself into the best physical shape of my life. I had one season of college baseball remaining to make my statement to the pro scouts. The previous summer was an education and a confidence-builder. This spring was going to be make it or break it.

I was in the gym constantly, playing handball alone or with whoever came by, slamming the hard little rubber ball all over the court, always in recovery the next day from the severe bruising along the fingers that was a painful but necessary part of the sport. A pitcher succeeds or fails with his legs, and I wanted mine to be ready for a strong season. Handball was an excellent sport for the legs, the constant side to side, forward and back movements required great stamina and leg strength over a two-hour session.

My major was in English/Education. I was on track to teach secondary school if my plans for a baseball career somehow failed to materialize. I didn't allow myself to consider the possibility.

That winter I was assigned to my student teaching requirement in Browerville, a small town just north of Long Prairie. I was learning how to get comfortable in front of a roomful of kids who were only a few years younger than me. I knew the material and I was enjoying the whole experience. The Browerville baseball coach heard that I was playing for St. John's and invited me to an early indoor practice to help with some instruction and start my own throwing program. I was happy to join them; the season couldn't start soon enough.

After a typical long Minnesota winter, it was wonderful to finally slip the Rawlings on my left hand and grip a baseball again. So I was soft-throwing in the gymnasium with the Browerville High School baseball team one late March afternoon when I heard a distinct "pop" during an easy toss to my catcher. I went to my knees; the pain in my right shoulder was intense. I asked for the ball and tried to throw again, but it was impossible. I headed back to the University for a diagnosis.

The doctor at St. John's examined my injured shoulder and determined I had separated it sometime that winter, probably playing handball. He recommended that I bind my arm to my side for ten days, rest it, limit all movement and see where it was after that. I followed orders; the season was beginning shortly and I had to be healthy.

Ten days later I removed the sling, gingerly rotated my arm and found no pain. I headed for the practice field and immediately began tossing the ball again, relieved and grateful that what had felt like a serious injury apparently was only a bump in the road. I had never had arm trouble other than the standard stiffness and soreness that was a normal part of a pitcher's weekly routine. I wasn't about to have problems now.

The next day at practice, Easy Ed came over to where I was throwing and said, "How does it feel?"

"Fine," I replied. And truthfully, it did.

"Good," he said, "Because you're starting tomorrow against Concordia."

I nodded and went back to throwing. A tiny nagging sliver of doubt tried to insinuate that maybe it was too soon; maybe I should give it another week and make sure all was well. But the coach told me I was going to play, and I wanted to play.

The next day I was back on the mound, the one place in the world I always felt completely comfortable and in control. I was cruising on a three-hitter into the seventh inning. We were up a couple of runs and I felt good and in charge and on my way to my first of what I knew would be many wins that year and a nice bonus from major league baseball for signing my first contract.

My catcher put down two fingers for a curve ball, I nodded, went into my windup, let go of the ball and ..."pop." The same sound I'd heard a couple weeks before, the same pain. I walked off the mound not knowing at the time that it would be the last game I'd ever play with a healthy right arm.

The next day I came down with a fever and a cold. I was very sick for a few days and, when I finally felt good enough, I experimented with a throwing motion, but to no avail. I tried tying my arm down again. No results. The pain was there and wasn't going away. My parents offered to pay for a trip to the team doctor for the Minnesota Twins. I made an appointment to see him, and a week later when I finally walked out of his office after a thorough examination, my world was a different place. He told me I had what he ominously termed "a dead arm." The fever had allowed the injury to become inflamed and, according to him, I had a "dry shoulder." A Twins relief pitcher had suffered a similar injury the year before and was now out of baseball. He told me I could undergo a series of cortisone shots, but he wouldn't recommend it. Rotator cuff surgery was rare in 1963.

I went back to St. John's determined to finish the season with my teammates. Easy Ed kept putting me out there on the mound, but to avoid the stabbing pain I had to shorten my throwing motion to the extent that I lost at least twenty miles per hour off my fastball and all the bite off my curve ball. I was easy meat for every team I'd been beating for three years. And they loved it.

I was twenty-one and it was time to get real about a career. Unbelievably, it wasn't going to involve professional baseball.

18

CANADA, EH?

Canada is a country so square that even the
female impersonators are women.
~ Richard Brenner

OUR EXPERIENCE IN TORONTO at Canada's
Wonderland, a theme park where performing under the roller
coaster required stopping the show for thirty seconds until the
coaster passed, convinced us that when Canadian crowds could
actually hear the routines; they loved us. So when the Vancouver
World's Fair asked us to spend a couple of weeks doing street theater
in '86, we jumped at the chance.

An old friend told us about a street festival in Edmonton that
was looking for unusual acts, so we booked ourselves into Summerfest
for another two weeks and set off for a summer in the hinterlands.

The Edmonton Street Festival was superb; most of the shows
took place on downtown streets. We were assigned a general area
and could strike up a show for the lunchtime office workers and
passersby.

One of the most unusual and uniquely skilled street performers at that time was Artis the Spoonman, a weird dude from the Seattle area who spread out a number of wooden spoons and silver utensils on a towel on the ground and turned himself into a percussion section.

Playing the "spoons" has a long history in American folk music, along with other found objects and everyday tools like the jug and washboard. Artis was later immortalized in a Soundgarden song, and Pete Seeger said of him, "He's the best spoon player in the whole damn universe." But for these two weeks he was entertaining the bankers and lawyers who were taking their lunches on the Edmonton mall.

Artis, like the rest of us, survived by passing the hat after his show. Frank Zappa once said to him, "You haven't got a commercial bone in your body." At that time in Edmonton, Artis was not only non-commercial, he was actively anti-capitalistic. I watched one performance when he'd gathered a large crowd of onlookers as he worked himself into a percussive lather, smacking his spoons into a frenzy of athletic rhythms and intricate beats and measures.

He often ended his show with a song that celebrated anarchy. Something like: "C'mon people, let's kill all the bankers, down with the system that exploits you and me, the brokers and lawyers who make all the money, etc., etc."

Joe pointed to the crowd and said, "Well, there goes his hat pass."

His audience, most of them nicely dressed in suits and ties, was thinning rapidly. Artis had set up his show right in front of a bank. But he knew exactly what he was doing; his smile of satisfaction told us all we needed to know. For Artis, it was never the money; it was a chance to make a statement.

Our show was less controversial, an Edmonton newspaper critic wrote: *They're a decidedly daft duo currently tickling many a funny bone at Summerfest. With their less-than-fancy sword work, rapier-like punning and broad physical humor, their comedy owes as much to Laurel and Hardy as it does to Avon's bard.*

Then it was on to Vancouver, where we were one of only six American street acts to entertain the international crowds at the World's Fair. We were bowled over with the quality and variety of street performers we worked with.

There was a Czechoslovakian stage combat troupe who performed a twenty-minute show with swords and staffs that was the best thing we'd ever seen. Their setup was a casual meeting of two rival groups of ruffians in a medieval tavern, and the subsequent battle. All was wordless. It was a purely physical confrontation, complete with astonishing athleticism, pratfalls, tumbles, and acrobatic leaps off tables and chairs onto concrete.

One of the Czech performers watched our show one afternoon came up to us afterwards and motioned to Joe to hand him one of our swords. He looked it over, waved it around for a moment, and then handed it back to Joe with a silent nod of approval.

One of the more memorable troupes performing in Vancouver that summer was a colorful entourage called Cirque du Soleil. They used large flags, streaming banners, boom-box music and otherworldly costumes to present a jaw-dropping half-hour of gymnastic excellence. Balancing, bodies flying through the air, gravity-defying feats of skill, all of it perfectly choreographed and presented with serious artistic fervor.

Joe and I were witnessing the first performances of the traveling act before it became a giant force on the international scene.

While I was zipping around Canada, my father began a battle for his life. Ben and Helen were happily retired from the restaurant business they built after leaving the farm.

Only the year before, on Dad's seventy-fifth birthday, I wrote a script and my brothers and sister and I roasted him by acting out scenes from his life. He was a very happy man that day and gave a heartfelt, off the cuff speech about the importance of family and how amazed he was to arrive intact to 1985.

But by that fall Dad's health was no longer strong. I dropped in on them in San Diego where they were spending the winter. I was in town doing a corporate show and was surprised to see this usually robust, rugged six-footer looking pale and tired. We talked for hours, a conversation I remember for its lack of self-consciousness.

Dad and I always seemed to be trying to break out of our father-son roles, and never quite succeeding. But that day was special. We simply talked and enjoyed each other.

We talked about him and his apparent difficulty in fully recovering from a recent heart surgery. But he wasn't complaining.

We talked about me and my family and how remarkable it was that I was making a living entertaining people. Mom joined in now and then, but even she seemed to sense that this was an important, long-delayed conversation between father and son.

By spring an x-ray revealed that Dad was in an advanced stage of prostate cancer – already metastasized to his bones. The family gathered at his bedside at the hospital one April night. Dad was cheerful and seemingly confident in his upcoming surgery the next morning. My eight-year-old son Peter gave him a "God's Eye" he made for Dad. We told jokes, laughed, and tried our best to keep everything as normal as we could. But the prognosis was not good; we all knew it, and so did he.

The next morning, we met in his room as they prepared him for surgery and, as he was wheeled out, Dad looked at all of us and smiled. A single tear rolled down his cheek and he said, "Goodbye."

We protested, "See you in a little while, Dad."

The surgery was successful, but Dad had a stroke during the surgery and was left in a deep coma. I was acting in a comedy in Minneapolis, and I traveled back and forth to sit by his bedside and stay with Mom. The rest of our family was in constant attendance.

Two weeks later, Dad died peacefully.

The parish priest later told us what Dad said to him the night before his surgery after the family left. "Father, I don't think I'm going to make it this time."

The priest asked how Dad felt about that and he said, "I'm okay with it."

My dad lost his father when he was a small child. He had five brothers and three sisters to help raise him. I am grateful to have had him around as long as I did. He led a truly remarkable life, plowing farm fields behind a team of horses as a child, surviving the Great Depression and the battles of the South Pacific, going through bankruptcy and coming out successfully on the other side, leaving a memorable legacy of hard work, faith, and devotion to his wife and children. His kids were his great pride and happiness, and he led by example and a firm hand that unfailingly inspired us to instant obedience and healthy respect.

Standing near his casket at the visitation the night before the funeral, one memory popped into my head that made me smile and silently whisper, "Thanks, Dad."

It happened on a hot day on the farm when I was sixteen. Dad and I were using crowbars, a tractor, and heavy chains to remove the large stones from a twenty-acre plot he intended to use for part of the corn crop.

We finished digging up and loading a two-hundred-pound rock onto the stone boat and were sweating and panting in the shade of the tractor wheel when he looked at me and asked, "Do you want to do this the rest of your life?"

"Absolutely not!"

"Then get an education."

No lecture, no big lesson. It was that simple. We moved on to the next stone. But I never forgot it. Thanks to him and Mom and their amazing work ethic, I haven't picked one rock out of a field since.

19

MOUSE DROPPINGS

Timon   *Who's the brains in this outfit?*
Pumbaa   *Uhh...*
Timon   *My point exactly.*
~ *The Lion King*

LATER THAT YEAR, Joe and I were trying to decide whether or not to accept an invitation from Expo '88 in Brisbane, Australia, to entertain the millions of visitors they were expecting. The Brisbane organizers found what they thought was the perfect sponsor for Puke & Snot: Foster's Beer. We would be well paid, housed and fed like actual human beings, and would in turn work a regular schedule of shows throughout the run of Expo '88. And, of course, we'd get an unlimited supply of Foster's. It seemed like a great way to spend a summer, but for some reason we put off making the decision until late spring of that year. And out of nowhere, the Mouse called.

Steve Hedrick was a talent booking agent working with Disney Creative in Orlando. Like many young executives on their way up in the Disney empire, he was an actor before he moved into management. His beautiful wife Diane had also been an actor and performer. Steve was tasked to book talent for a summer variety show at a relatively undeveloped piece of Disney property consisting of a few shops and restaurants, a Disney souvenir outlet, and an outdoor stage near the water called the Dock.

The Disney marketeers wanted to attract more people to this area to shop and get rid of whatever small change might be left after spending the day and most of their vacation budget at the theme parks. Live entertainment from five to nine each evening was their solution.

Mr. Hedrick had seen us at the Sarasota Medieval Faire and thought I could help him identify some acts to work through the summer. It was late spring and I knew that most of the good shows were already booked for the season; but I sent out a call for videos from various people working waterfronts, malls, streets, and alleys across the nation. I received twenty videos in less than a week, sent them off to Hedrick and waited for a response.

Steve selected seven acts from the bunch, booked most of them for two or three weeks and offered Joe and me a lot of work that summer. He paid well, seemed to be the kind of guy who kept his promises and inspired confidence that the Disney organization was just possibly not the evil empire we heard it was.

Joe and I had a decision to make: a summer drinking Foster's on the far side of the planet and becoming honorary Australians at Expo '88, or travel down to Orlando and add the Disney name to our thin resume. It came down to money, as it often did, so we stayed in the States to work with the Mouse with the deep pockets.

An old friend from the early festival days in Minnesota sold the idea of interactive street theater to the Disney Company some years before, and by this time had more than forty performers working various locations at EPCOT and MGM. Herbie Hansen had gone from the paths and lanes of Renaissance festivals to the sidewalks of Disney, and not so coincidentally turned himself into a well-paid entrepreneur.

We had visions of a similar career path. Not exactly Las Vegas, but we knew Disney could be a virtual black hole for live entertainment. They sucked up anything that came within their gravitational field. We were ready to roll the dice with Dis.

I flew to Orlando and rented a three-bedroom condo within twenty minutes of Disney World. I wanted "my actors" to have a decent place to stay while they toiled in the Florida humidity. I charged everyone twelve dollars a day; they had their own bedrooms and the use of the condo, pool, and all the amenities. This paid the rent and allowed me to bring my family.

Working for Disney was a revelation. We had all heard the horror stories about long hours, small compensation, and ridiculous rules about dress codes and facial hair. One of our friends, a giant of a man with a voice that sounded like Orson Welles on steroids, had been hired at several festivals to play the king. He had a spectacular beard, one he groomed carefully and was rightfully proud of.

Disney asked him to join their street troupe where he was asked to develop a variety of characters at the MGM Park. There was only one hitch: he had to shave his beard. Disney would provide him with a costume beard if any of his characters needed one, but employee facial hair was against Disney policy and wouldn't be tolerated. He agreed, shaved his luxurious whiskers, and the next time I saw him he was playing an Arabian prince in the "Aladdin" parade, with a full fake beard that didn't look half as good as his original.

These were the kinds of Disney decisions we had heard about. But our first night on the Dock Stage a light rain began after our first show. An announcement came instantly over the sound system: "Ladies and gentlemen, the shows this evening will be postponed until the weather system has cleared the area. We'll mop the stage, dry the seats and continue with the show when we get the all-clear from the weatherman. Thanks, and enjoy your evening."

Joe looked at me. "Holy shit, you mean we don't have to work in the rain?"

"Apparently not."

"I love this place!"

A small army of Disney employees converged on the area and began mopping, squee-geeing, wiping and swabbing. We'd been used to Renaissance festivals that required acts to get out there and do the show, period. Tornadoes? So what? Raining? The ticket says "rain or shine." Lightning? Put that metal sword over your head and entertain these people; they drove all the way from Nebraska fer chrissake. And here was a producer who not only paid our rate without whining, but actually seemed concerned about the safety and comfort of the performers!

Joe and I went backstage and quietly wept at our good fortune, our tears of gratitude easily raising the water level of our little Disney pond two inches. We only did one show that night, the rain stopped at nine P.M., too late for us to go back out there. It happened a lot that summer. Nice gig.

If adventure has a name, it must be...

Indiana Snot and the Temple of Dolts

As the summer progressed, we began to see some of the same people coming back night after night. There was an affable older gentleman in a floppy blue fishing cap; he showed up twice a week and sat in the fourth row on the aisle. He waved and pointed down the row to show us the new batch of seniors he brought in on the bus to see us each night. We talked to him after one of the shows and found out he loved the vaudeville style of the show. He was bringing new people each night from the senior high rise where he lived, to share the jokes with them.

One night an old friend of Joe's appeared backstage and took him over to Captain Jack's for a little food and conversation. Ninety minutes later, Joe returned with a pleasant glow that I knew immediately spelled big trouble for our next appearance. We were introduced, started the show and, within two minutes, Joe was looking at me like he'd never heard the lines before.

We stumbled through the show. The sword fights were a near disaster; Joe could barely function. When we got offstage I turned on him like a rabid badger.

"You had to have a couple of beers, right?"

"Just one."

"Just one my ass; you're drunk."

"No, I'm not."

"Bullshit! There were Disney suits in that audience, and you could barely remember what show we were doing. It was embarrassing. You nearly took off my ear with the sword fight. If you ever have a drink between shows again, it will be the final appearance of Puke & Snot with you in it. *You can't drink and do comedy. It doesn't work, you idiot!*"

Joe took me at my word and never had another drink before a show.

Johnny Fox, the only sword swallower I know

Arsene Dupin with hideous chapeau

The long, hot Orlando summer proceeded apace, with appearances by Waldo and Woodhead, Murph the Physical Comedian, Johnny Fox the Sword Swallower, and Arsene Dupin from Paris. We hung by the pool and headed into Orlando at night to shoot pool. Johnny entertained bystanders by unscrewing a two-piece cue and swallowing the skinnier half; Arsene would grab five pool balls and juggle them, to the amazement of the guys at the next table.

Eating dinner with these boys was always a questionable proposition. Spoons were bent, those little coffee creamers were used as props to perform eye-gouging feats of grisly comedy and the show never stopped.

Johnny and Arsene were old friends and friendly rivals, often accusing each other of stealing the other's best bits. Listening to them argue about who was the first one to do the "lit cigarette in the mouth" bit was like hearing two old ladies argue about recipes. Two old ladies who swore like pirates.

But Hedrick's cast of oddball performers became the show to see that summer in the Disney parks. By the end of August the place was packed every night for the three featured acts on the schedule. The next time I talked to Steve, he'd been kicked upstairs and made an actual Disney producer.

Shortly thereafter, he convinced Michael Eisner that Buffalo Bill's Wild West Show was just what was needed in the new European Disney World, and he left with his wife and kids to become the American general manager of Disney World/Paris. I like to think Puke & Snot helped him get there. We didn't, but as Gore Vidal once said, "Whenever a friend succeeds, a little something in me dies."

We continued our relationship with Mickey and his minions through the next few years, but there was never a realistic opportunity to branch out into other areas of their conglomerate like our buddy

Herbie did. It was 2001 before we returned to the Magic Kingdom, this time as "Perry and Slice," two pirate characters in the plaza outside the Pirates of the Caribbean ride, who entertained passing crowds with fifteen-minute shows six days a week.

An old Disney friend of ours was now the creative manager for the Magic Kingdom. He had been adding variety entertainment all over the park. He called one day and said, "I think it might be time to bring back the two guys with the unmarketable names."

I said, "You know we can't re-write enough of this show to make your job safe if your boss doesn't think dick jokes in the Magic Kingdom are appropriate."

"Don't worry about it; I'm pretty close to retirement and I think it'll be fine. Just tweak it a little; it goes by so fast, nobody'll notice."

So we agreed to come in and do two weeks, just to see if everybody liked us enough to sign us to a longer contract.

With the exception of the twenty-year-old Disney audio system that never functioned properly, the show worked just fine.

The largely international crowds didn't always understand the fast-paced double entendres; but they seemed to really enjoy the slapstick and the swordplay. We'd do fifteen minutes, pose for pictures, sign the kid's autograph books like we'd seen Mickey and Goofy do many times, and head back to the dressing room to change out of our soaked shirts and do it all again an hour later.

Our dressing room was blocks away above the Frontierland Music Hall. We had to negotiate the tunnels beneath the park to get there. We shared the dressing room space with five young acrobats from Kenya who were also doing six or seven shows a day in the Adventureland Plaza.

They ranged in age from eighteen to twenty-three. They performed astonishingly athletic acrobatic routines barefoot on the concrete in the plaza, risking their lives (it seemed to us) while flying through the air over, under, and around their counterparts. They told us they were one of several teams of Kenyans working around the U.S., and that they were sending back as much money as they could to their families in Kenya.

They had experienced some pretty distasteful and blatantly racist treatment from some long-time Disney musicians who, according to the Kenyans, complained that they "smelled" and needed to "learn English." It was a side of working at Disney I hadn't expected to see, and when we learned a week later that the whole Magic Kingdom band had been summarily fired, we didn't get too worked up about it. What goes around…

We managed to survive two weeks before we told our Disney producer that it would take more money than he wanted to pay to keep our show going in the Caribbean Plaza for the six-month contract he proposed. I think they were relieved, partly because they couldn't decide if "poop deck" jokes were what they wanted as the public face of the Magic Kingdom.

"Perry & Slice" in the Magic Kingdom, Orlando

20

THE RETURN OF MR. BILL

*There are three primal urges in human beings: food, sex,
and re-writing someone else's play.*
~ Romulus Linney, playwright

JOE AND I WERE NEVER INTERESTED in playwriting, whether ours or re-writing anyone else's. But at one point we inadvertently helped re-write someone else's life. In the late nineties, as Joe and I were passing the hat after a performance at the Minnesota festival, a middle-aged man dropped a bill into my cup and said, "Nice show, Sieve."

I recognized the voice, but not the guy who owned it. Until he smiled. The unmistakable grin was the same one I had seen onstage that first night at St. John's many years before when I watched the skinny freshman classmate convulse an auditorium full of strangers. It was Bill the Actor. Except I was actually talking to Bill the Lawyer. He was exactly the same guy I remembered, with less hair, a law degree, and an additional fifty pounds.

Standing in the shade trying to catch up on thirty years in a few minutes, we decided to have lunch when he was back in Minneapolis. He had a successful law practice in Duluth and traveled a lot, but wanted to get together to talk.

The following week, we met for lunch and Bill the Solicitor briefly sketched his resume since those early days in the sixties: he had left St. John's, enrolled in law school at Catholic University and had been an extremely successful trial lawyer, both for the prosecution and for the defense, ever since.

The stage presence that served him so well in those lead roles for Father Dominic made him a formidable courtroom advocate. He knew how to play that role; he felt he could hypnotize any jury put in front of him. I was not surprised, remembering clearly how precise and convincing he was onstage and how those audiences hung on his every line. Then he surprised me.

He said, "I've been a lawyer for almost thirty years, but when I saw you up there on that stage doing that show, I knew that's what I wanted to do again. I want to go back to acting, and I'm thinking about quitting my law practice and doing it."

I was nonplused. "Have you talked to your wife about it? What does your family think?"

"My wife says if I do she'll divorce me."

"Sounds reasonable to me."

I laughed and thanked him for the compliment. This was a guy who'd been a consummate actor and at eighteen possessed all the skills and chops of someone twice his age – and he was seriously telling me that the Puke & Snot Show inspired him to dump his chosen career in law and go back onstage as an under-appreciated actor. Good Lord, was he kidding?

Apparently not. The next time we had lunch, he proudly informed me that he was doing Willy Loman in *Death of a Salesman* at the Duluth Playhouse. He invited me to see it.

I said, "What about your law practice?"

"Oh, I quit."

"And your wife?

"She divorced me."

I always hoped that our little show was a positive force, a ray of sunshine, a sturdy fortress of silliness and laughter that might for just a moment shield our faithful audiences from the slings and arrows of everyday life; a show that might, with the help of stupefying amounts of alcohol, anesthetize someone who had, for example, just lost his life savings at the roulette table.

I never wanted it to be...*that.*

Chuckles amid the financial ruins

21

JACKS BE NIMBLE

If at first you don't succeed, try, try again. Then quit.
No use being a damn fool about it.
~ W.C. Fields

THAT FINAL SPRING at St. John's as my senior class prepared to leave the protective shelter of the deep woods and enter the real world of work and responsibility, many of us who spent four years seeking competition every waking moment were going through a strange kind of withdrawal. We were preoccupied with inventing as many new ways to compete as we could.

As seniors, we had just achieved the first national championship St. John's had ever claimed, a football victory over Prairie View A & M in Sacramento in January that threw our little school into a paroxysm of pride. We decided that one national championship was not enough; there were still a few months left in our college careers; there could be more. Somebody decided that the children's game of jacks had no known national team champion; so a few of us traveled to a toy store and picked up several sets of jacks and the small rubber balls that accompany them and began to practice on the smooth tile floors of our dormitories.

Within a few days, jacks games were breaking out all over campus. 270-pound defensive tackles were on their knees in hallways yelling, "Foursies!" and "Eggs in a basket!"

I happily joined my compadres, doggedly determined to salvage something of value from my injury-dominated senior year. Quickly, I became a college jacks player good enough to make the team and compete against St. Catherine's, a sister college from St. Paul that had thrown down a dainty glove for our first match, and we had accepted. They showed up and were stunned when we easily defeated them with an ease and skill level they hadn't expected from a group of knuckle-dragging frat boys. We accepted their invitation to a rematch on their campus, and a week later I accompanied a select few players to St. Paul to defend our self-declared "national jacks championship."

On game day we were pleased to see local Twin Cities TV reporters and newspapers in attendance as we faced off with a determined-looking team of "Katies" on a freshly polished marble floor in the student center. Apparently, our reputation as the self-proclaimed national jacks champs was taken seriously by the press. This was what we had hoped for. We were, you understand, *champions*. The media needed to watch our every move.

An hour later, our dreams of further glory were ended by an adept left-handed blonde who wrested the championship banner from our grasp. She was just too quick. It was over. We gave up our trophy gracefully, and headed back to the woods. Graduation was approaching, all the games were ending and it was time to get out there in the marketplace and find a job, and, if possible, a good Catholic girl with freshly repaired teeth and a new winter coat.

22

GARGLING AT THE
FOUNTAIN OF KNOWLEDGE

He who can, does. He who cannot, teaches.
~ George Bernard Shaw

He who shall, so shall he who.
~ Ralph Puke

THE SUMMER OF 1964 I signed a contract to teach high school English and speech at a small high school in southern Minnesota, the superintendent sweetening the deal with a long list of extra-curricular activities I would supervise that added a significant amount of money to my salary package.

I was to teach five classes of senior English and speech, direct three high school plays including the contest one-act, direct all contest speech activities, coach the baseball team and assist in coaching junior high basketball. For this I would receive an additional five hundred dollars to add to my base salary of $4700 for the school year. I was in hog heaven.

I plunged headlong into my chosen profession. I was twenty-one and about to make a difference. I loved the classroom, the idea that I might know something that was worth imparting to younger ears, but it wasn't long before my boyish idealism would be tempered with the realpolitik of rural Minnesota public education.

I found out shortly after I began teaching that the head baseball job I accepted had been held by a teacher still on the faculty, and one whom the community loved and respected. Ray was also a pretty damn good coach, having taken the little school to a couple of state tournaments in his fifteen-year career. He had asked the superintendent for a twenty-five dollar raise to coach that season, which would have brought his salary to a whopping fifty dollars for the spring. The superintendent turned him down and for good measure hired me for seventy-five dollars.

When I found out, I felt terrible, like an interloper. I immediately regretted taking the job, but Ray liked me and graciously told me to forget it and do my best.

Later that year I volunteered to serve on the salary arbitration committee and, with five other idealists, spent hours hammering out what we all felt was an excellent contract proposal for the school board's consideration. When the day came to meet with the board, all five of us were ushered in to the board room to sit on short folding chairs around a large conference table, our heads barely poking up above the level of the shiny cherry surface, while the board members perched properly in their comfortably upholstered matching chairs and listened politely for five minutes as we presented our case for a small increase in both salary and career steps for the coming year.

They took our proposal under advisement, dismissed us and promptly tossed our hard work into the trash. Days later we learned that an agreement had been reached with Chuck, our committee head. No raise, no increase in the steps, no further consideration, no more meetings.

Stunned, I walked in to Chuck's classroom the next morning and asked him what happened. He patiently explained to the rookie teacher that there was no way the board would approve our proposal; "You have to get real, son. I live in this town and know these people. The board chairman is a veterinarian and thinks we're all paid too much already. He wants to limit a teacher's career steps to no more than six or seven years because he doesn't want teachers to stay in the community for long; they get too expensive. We got a deal; let it be."

Gladly wolde he lerne, and gladly teche.

I was an English teacher, but the math was simple. By the time I reached the doddering age of twenty-seven, I would be at the top salary level on that faculty. No further compensation necessary, thank you for your service. I had been under the impression that teachers were valued and even revered members of their communities, that good ones were rare, and that hard work would be recognized and compensated accordingly.

Never saw that coming. Fast ball down the middle. Strike *one*.

Plunge back into the work, boy, you're paying your bills, to hell with them; your students appreciate you and love your classes; you're hitting them out of the park every day, it's a good job, summers off, plenty of vacation.

Three years later I was stirring the pot at another high school in southwestern Minnesota. It only took ten teachers to create a union local in 1967. After a particularly acrimonious teacher's meeting with the previous year's secretary of the local Minnesota Education Association, the Minimum Ten met with the Minnesota Federation of Teachers and were granted union representation and support.

We held informational meetings for the community and patiently explained that nothing would change in the contract, that we were the same teachers they'd always had, but that we were now represented by a teacher's union that reserved the right to strike if a proper balance of power between teachers and administration wasn't achieved.

This news hit the small farm town like an earthquake. People called the school office daily and howled about "those damn unions" taking over their high school. I was teaching speech and English, and vocally supporting some of my best students who were challenging the school policy of suppressing student discussion of anything to do with the Vietnam War, which was raging at the time.

Since many of them were nearly draft age and had their lives on the line, I told them that it was their country; they certainly had a right to ask questions of their advisors who were insisting they limit student-council discussions to homecoming dance decorations and cheerleader uniforms.

The principal, a crew-cut nasty by the name of Fischke, and his buddy the school counselor, a bald dunce of a chemistry teacher named Phelt, determined that I was a dangerous influence on their charges and someone to be watched.

Dress codes and hair length were big subjects at this tiny school. One morning the Dynamic Duo, Fischke and Phelt, stepped unannounced into my second-hour American literature class, each holding a ruler, and proceeded to stroll up and down the aisles, stopping to measure a boy's hair and, if it was deemed too long, sending him immediately to the local barber; commanding selected girls to kneel beside their desks; if their skirts didn't reach completely to the floor, sending them home to change clothes. I watched the little drama unfold from my desk in the front of the room, weighing my options. This could not stand.

I followed them into the hallway, loudly pointing out the irony of a bald guy and his crew-cut accomplice measuring hair length on eighteen-year-old men and told them both to stay the hell out of my classroom for the rest of the year. The class applauded as I returned, but I knew the battle lines were drawn.

The school establishment immediately lined up to make my life as difficult as possible. The cooks in the lunch room would see me coming down the line and hand me a plate with a noticeably smaller portion of the church-lady goulash.

The first time I thought it was a coincidence. But it happened every day. The day I was given a chicken wing instead of the full quarter chicken everyone else was served, I laughed and refused to move until someone filled up my plate. A tense standoff, lasting no more than thirty seconds, but the hair-netted harpies backed down and reluctantly gave me my man-sized chunk of chicken, accompanied by normal portions of tired vegetables and gray potatoes.

This juvenile harassment went on all year. One evening in the middle of a rehearsal for the senior class spring play, the lights went out in the auditorium where my cast was working. I turned around and the janitor was hauling away the scaffold where the spotlights were mounted.

"You have to leave, it's nine o'clock."

"Please leave those lights where they are; we've got the auditorium till ten tonight."

"I have to get home, you have to leave."

I trotted back and grabbed the scaffold. A brief struggle, I was younger, stronger and more pissed off. He let go and said, "I'm going to report this to the superintendent."

"Please do," I replied, "He'll want to know who's working and who's going home early."

Sometime in April, contracts were stuffed into our mailboxes and, as we opened our envelopes in the faculty lounge, I saw that my pink—literally, a bright-pink—slip was badly written but succinct: *At a meeting of the Board of Education on March 12, by a vote of 6-0, it was determined that you will not be offered a contract for the coming school year. Reason being a conflict of philosophy on Americanism.*

Curve ball on the corner, nice pitch, strike *two*.

Ah, Americanism. Some practice it; others preach it, and still others have no idea what the hell it is. I certainly didn't. But I could see where this was headed. I was a teacher; this was my job and chosen profession. Someone had decided that they were going to screw with me in a very significant way by messing with my livelihood.

I sat there, staring at the piece of paper, wondering if I truly was a bad teacher, an unsavory influence, a loose cannon. A quick survey of the lounge told me that I was the only fired teacher present. Apparently, I was a bad apple.

I did a quick mental review of that year: the publishing of my letter to the editor in the county daily paper, supporting student's right to speak out on issues affecting them; the hairless chemistry teacher telling his classes he knew for sure that I was a communist; the April night I knocked on the door of the social studies teacher's house for our weekly poker game and was met by Vern's smiling face and his greeting, "Hey, come in, did you hear the news? They got him."

"Got who?" I hadn't heard.

"King. They killed the son of a bitch. Come on in. The beer's in the fridge; we're just getting started."

Martin Luther King? Killed? My teacher friends at the poker table were silent, looking at me as if to say, "Yeah, they killed Martin Luther King; but do you want to talk politics or play poker?"

I was speechless, and not just at the news of King's death. I thought I knew old Vern. I played a few hands, excused myself and left the game.

No, it wasn't me. I had stumbled into a bizarre community that shared few of my values or beliefs, a Stephen King-like fantasy small town where life was ordinary, conventional, placid on the surface – but open the wrong door and the Lizard People would tear your throat out. Vern the Reptile King. Excellent and jolly poker player, told a good joke, but show him a black person and he grew fangs, turned green and left a slime trail into the night.

Time to line up some interviews for a better job in a more enlightened environment. My girlfriend's brother was the personnel director of a large suburban high school outside Minneapolis and asked me to apply. He thought I'd be a lively addition to his teaching staff; no time like the present.

St. John's sent him my personnel file and we arranged a meeting. The following week I drove to Osseo, Minnesota, and met with Bruce, girlfriend Bonnie's talented brother. He liked me; this would be a piece o' cake, a slam dunk years before the term was coined.

He welcomed me into his office, sat down and held up a blue booklet. He'd just received my file, but there was something in it that would make it impossible for me to get a teaching job anywhere. He couldn't show it to me or tell me who had placed the poisoned letter in my professional file; it would be "unethical." But if that letter remained, I was unemployable.

Lyndon Johnson had signed the Freedom of Information Act two years before, but its effects hadn't yet trickled down to the education establishment; teachers had no right to know what was in their files or who might have fixed them. I left my girlfriend's brother's office in a state of shock.

On the drive back, I remembered my old friend Chuck from my first year of teaching. My golfing buddy was now the principal of a high school in another small burg. I called him – Chuck old boy, I don't want to work for you but I do want you to get my file and tell me who's trying to blackball me.

Three days later, the phone rang. It was Chuck.

"Well, what's in it?"

"It's bad, young man, in this business we fill out a form. We give teachers check marks from excellent to poor in a dozen categories and write our evaluation at the end. This guy gave you "fair-to-poor" on everything and wrote nothing. That's code; it means 'call me about this guy.' It's our way of keeping bad teachers moving and hopefully out of the profession. If I call him he'll tell me not to hire you. Want me to call him?"

"Who is it?"

"It's the superintendent at your current school."

"Thanks, no need to call him; I know what I have to do."

I drove back to my little town Sunday night and prepared for my morning assault on Alan Flescher, a mousy little guy whom I'd barely spoken to but who apparently had decided, without ever being in my classroom, that I was a dangerous man. The following morning I arrived early, walked directly to the main office, "I need to speak to Mr. Flescher."

His secretary, "I'm sorry, Mr. Flescher is in a meeting."

I moved to his door. "I need to see him immediately."

"Sir, you can't go in there."

I walked in, Mr. Flescher was having his morning meeting with a donut, a cup of coffee, and a newspaper, with his nicely polished Tom McCanns resting on his desk.

"Good morning, Mr. Sieve, please sit down."

"No thanks, I'll stand."

I then delivered the best performance of my life, a piece of acting that in later years I would draw on whenever my character needed to plumb the depths of Lear-like rage. In retrospect, it was actually a fairly coherent five-minute improvised monologue. All the pent-up frustration of dealing with these people throughout the long school year flooded all over his desk.

I yelled; I swore. I paced melodramatically up and down. I pounded and sent pencils flying. I told him I found out what he did, that I didn't want to teach in his rat-hole of a school anyway. But I wasn't about to let him stop me from teaching in some other rat-hole of my own choosing. I had arrived at his little piss-pot town with an excellent reputation and I would most certainly leave with that reputation intact. I told him the state teacher's union was behind me (it was); we were prepared to sue him, the school board, every school employee including the school counselor who had publicly called me a commie, every snake who practiced racial hatred outside his social studies classes, every good American who tried to steal my spotlights, refused to feed me properly or "forgot" to clean my classroom, and that his picture would be on the front page of the county daily – that my parents were friends of the publisher (they weren't) and were wealthy enough (they weren't) to pursue him through the courts forever, and that all I wanted from him to avoid all this unpleasantness was a replacement recommendation put in my file by the time I interviewed at another school the following week.

I handed him his phone and said, "Call St. John's and have them send you the forms. Now! I'll wait."

He did, on the spot, squeaking that he had no memory of what he'd done but would certainly correct any "mistakes."

When I left his office, wiping the foam off my chin with my handkerchief, a small group of anxious office secretaries were huddled against the far wall, trying to decide whether or not to call the police. I felt much better. I had at least aired it all out, spoken my piece, defended myself, and maybe even scared the little shit a little.

Five days later, I was seated in the superintendent's office of a small high school in central Minnesota. The super had given me a tour of the school, showed me the classroom where I'd be working, offered me some extracurricular activities to pad my income and started paging through the ominous blue booklet that I recognized immediately as my file.

He stopped for a moment and silently read one of the records. I held my breath for a couple of heartbeats and he said, "You have an excellent file here, Mr. Sieve ... in fact, Mr. Flescher thinks very highly of you."

He'd selected, out of more than twenty files, Superintendent Shitbird's new "recommendation," and it was apparently a beaut. My performance had indeed been well received by my audience of one. It had an emotional impact, what all we artists hope and pray our work will achieve.

"Yes," I nodded. "Mr. Flescher and I have a good working relationship."

My next two years were delightful and full of amazing and memorable moments. I found a dedicated faculty and a supportive community, decided to start a theater, and directed *The Odd Couple* as the inaugural show.

To cast it, I went to a Friday night football game, asked people I knew along the rope line if they wanted to be in a play, handed them scripts, and started rehearsals a week later. I made some lifelong friends in that city, but, as the old saying goes, there were some flyspecks in the pepper.

One morning before school started a student came running into my class yelling "Come quick, it's Mr. Olson!"

I ran down the hall to his classroom to find Dan, a fellow teacher, giving the history teacher Jim Olson CPR. But it was obvious it was too late. There was a small pool of blood on the floor next to his desk. He had apparently had a heart attack and hit his head when he fell. The cut over his eye was no longer bleeding. His wife, who also taught in an adjoining wing, stood there still in her coat and scarf, watching the futile attempt to save his life.

The superintendent arrived, stared for a moment as Dan kept trying to revive him, then put his arm around Mrs. Olson and said, "I'll go back to the office and check on the insurance."

That startled me. I remember thinking *hmmm*, not the most sensitive thing a person could say to comfort a woman watching her husband die. The firemen arrived and tried to revive Jim, to no avail. We all went back to our classrooms as they placed a blanket over his lifeless body and waited for the ambulance.

I told my class what happened and we waited for the intercom announcement that school would be dismissed in honor of Mr. Jim Olson, a long-time cherished educator and good friend. No announcements. The minutes passed, the bell rang, and classes moved to the second period. Jerry the shop teacher, long and angular, with darting eyes and a military crew-cut, showed up at my door and motioned me outside to the hallway.

"What's happening, Jerry?"

"The reason there hasn't been an announcement is they're going to keep classes in session till one o'clock so they can get state aid—if they dismiss early, they lose it. And—this is unbelievable—I think they're planning to teach a class next period in Jim's room."

"Are you kidding?"

"I'm serious. They've mopped up the blood, the floor isn't even dry and I heard Mitchell is going to teach his class. Does your key open his room?"

"I think so."

"Go lock it and stand outside; don't let anybody in. I'll be there in a minute to back you up. No more business as usual, this is bullshit. If I ever die in this town I hope I die in an alley where at least they won't be stepping over my body on their way to work."

I headed down the hall. Jim's classroom was empty, a freshly mopped wet spot where his head had rested moments before. I locked the door and stood outside.

Within minutes, Mitchell the Peter Principal came hurrying up and asked, "Do you have a key to this door?"

"Yes, but I'm not opening it."

He exploded. "Goddammit, this is sentimental crap! You people have no idea what we have to do here. We have a school to run and his class will be here next period, I'm going to teach it; now open that door."

"Take his class to the gym if you need to, Mitch, nobody's teaching a class in this room until the floor dries. And it won't be dry till tomorrow. Nobody gets in today."

Jerry showed up and took up his spot next to me. We stood together; no one spoke. Mitchell finally turned away, muttering his way back down the hallway, and I realized I was shaking, whether from anger, fear, or a realization that, yes, I could be Jim Olson and somewhere down a longer road this could easily be my curtain call, a damp spot on a tile floor with some guy in a bad suit checking on the insurance.

At one P.M. the intercom crackled to life with the announcement that school buses would be arriving soon, an early dismissal to honor Mr. Olson sent everyone home early. Jerry walked by my classroom, looked in and shook his head.

Strike *three*. Slider, low and away. I'm outta here.

The career to which I dedicated my energies the past seven years suddenly seemed like a mistake. It was time to get out of town once again; time to scratch the itch to stand onstage somewhere and be the center of attention. I moved to Minneapolis to become an actor and take up residence in a red Naugahyde booth at Jimmy Hegg's.

23

WORKING SOLO

I look at my friendship with her as like having a gall stone.
You deal with it; there is pain, and then you pass it.
~ Sandra Bernhard on Madonna

THE PHONE RANG AT 5:30 one Saturday morning in September 1990. I picked it up; it was Joe. "We might have a problem. I'm in the emergency room at Fairview."

"No shit—what happened?"

"I don't know, but I'm on a gurney, I can't sit up, they think it might be kidney stones. If this keeps up, there's no way I'll be at the festival today."

"I'll be right there. Don't move."

"No problem, I can't."

I got dressed and headed to the hospital. There was Joe, on his side in the fetal position, sweating and in major pain. I tried to loosen him up: "What tickles?"

"My testicles – don't make me laugh; this is bad. They're gonna try and zap the kidney stones, whatever that means. What'll we do about the show?"

"Don't worry about the show; I'll think of something. Just get healthy enough to do the fest tomorrow."

I left him to the tender mercies of the guys in the white jackets.

Must think. Must come up with a way to pass the hat today without doing the shows…

By the time I pulled up in front of my house at 6:30, I had a plan. When I got to the festival, I told our long-time stage manager Daryl to be ready with Joe's microphone; I was going to audition new Snots today.

People started arriving forty-five minutes before the first show. By the time the Raspyni Brothers finished the opening half-hour, we were packed. Our trusty stage manager Daryl did his usual pre-show announcements and introduced Puke & Snot.

I walked out onstage and took a leap of faith: "Ladies and gentlemen, I have good news and bad news."

On cue, the crowd responded: "What's the good news?"

"The good news is that Snot is in the hospital."

Silence.

"Go ahead; ask me what the bad news is."

"What's the bad news?"

"The bad news is the Puke & Snot show will go on as scheduled. [NERVOUS LAUGHTER] I've always worried about what would happen if Snot left the show. What would I do for work? How would I pay my bills? Then it came to me—I need a *spare* Snot; and there's no time like the present."

I moved down off the stage and started up the center aisle.

"I need to audition new Snots. I need to find just the right guy, somebody with that familiar vacant stare, who looks kinda like an axe murderer, somebody who women might find interesting at first but with whom they'd never consider a serious relationship, somebody who ... you, sir! Come up on stage with me, you're the first actor we're going to audition today for the role of a lifetime!"

Daryl met us onstage, pinned the microphone on his shirt. I handed the guy the "Magaga Routine," one of our most recognizable sketches, and told him to just relax and read Snot's lines. Our first "actor" was a guy from Winona, Minnesota, named George.

George had a tough time pronouncing "magaga" at first, but quickly got into it and the crowd followed us. At one point, he delivered a Snot line, got a laugh and said, "Hey, this is funny stuff!" –which got a bigger laugh.

George was hooked on comedy. We got through that show. People were asking for Puke and George shirts, and I knew we'd be fine. Except for the final audition of the day when I picked a heavily tattooed biker out of the audience and, embarrassingly, he couldn't read.

Joe called later that night. He was back on his feet and would be there the next day. I told him we no longer needed him; George from Winona was willing to work for a lot less. Joe was not amused.

In his thirty-four years as Snot, Joe missed only one day of performances, that painful morning when his stones wouldn't allow him to stand up. But Puke & George & Bob & Steve & Randy & Don did five shows that day.

24

FEATHERLESS PARROTS

Oscar Wilde   *I wish I'd said that.*

James Whistler   *You will, Oscar; you will.*

ORIGINALITY IS IN SHORT SUPPLY in variety entertainment. Everybody seems to keep one eye out for a clever bit they can borrow and add to their own show. Jugglers are constantly watching each other for new ideas on keeping objects airborne and what to say about it while they're doing it. Fire eaters, magicians, and comics all seem to be able to recycle the same punch lines over and over, while either unaware or unconcerned that the line came from somewhere else.

The guiding principle seems to be: "If the author isn't in this audience, I'm gold."

Fred Allen once said of Milton Berle, who was infamous for stealing other comedian's lines, "He's done everybody's act. He's a parrot with skin on."

Renaissance festivals are rife with naked parrots.

In the earliest days of our tenure at the Minnesota festival, another performer warned us that two cast members were doing our material in a sword fight on the other side of the grounds. We put a quick stop to it, but kept an eye on them the rest of the run and threatened broken bones if they did it again.

Some years later we were in the middle of a show at the Minnesota festival when I noticed one of the members of a now-famous juggling troupe watching us. He was holding a notepad and pencil. After the show I walked over to him and said, "Hi Randy, good to see you. Taking notes?"

He laughed, "No, just some addresses here."

A few months later I was in my bathroom, shaving, when my wife called me into the living room where she was watching the jugglers on PBS in one of their "Shakespearean" productions from the Goodman Theater in Chicago. "You'd better watch this," she said.

I immediately heard Puke & Snot dialogue coming from two of the characters in *The Comedy of Errors*. Sad, I thought. Especially since these guys were regarded on the early festival circuit as the most original and inventive juggling troupe in the country.

Penn Jillette told a story of another guy doing his show word-for-word in a club in Philadelphia when Penn was just getting some notoriety as a young performer. Penn's solution: instead of challenging the thief, Penn simply went to the club owner and offered him two weeks of free shows if the owner would never hire the guy again and tell other owners not to hire him. According to Penn, it worked. The guy was instantly unemployable.

Penn's problem has always been that's he's a bit too creative and a bit too original. He comes up with material that other performers find impossible not to repeat. Write a mediocre show and you solve that problem.

The nakedest parrot I ever saw appeared on the same stage Joe and I were working at the Sarasota Medieval Faire. Johnny Fox, Joe, and I were sitting around backstage in the warm March sun on the grounds of the Ringling Museum while a young juggler was working onstage. We were reminiscing about the old days of the Ringling, when it was new and fresh and an event that John and Mabel would have been proud to host on their estate.

As we talked, I heard something very familiar, words and phrases I had listened to many times before. I looked at Joe. He was frowning; he was hearing the same thing.

"Is that what I think it is?"

"Yes. It's Penn's old juggling routine."

Fox listened, but wasn't sure. Joe and I were. We had listened to Penn do his shtick from the beginning; whoever it was onstage was doing it word-for-word, inflection-for-inflection. I looked out at a tall young performer doing the best impression of Penn Jillette I'd ever seen.

As we listened, he was wrapping it up with Penn's fire-eating routine, with the signature admonishment to the audience that was pure Penn & Teller: "As I eat this fire and you watch me do it, I don't want you to ask yourself how I'm doing it. I want you to ask yourself *why*."

It was the line Penn used to close their stage show as he ate fire in a nearly darkened theater, and as he'd snuff out the last flame in his mouth, the theater went completely black and applause rang out. We had seen the show several times, and here was this guy doing it exactly as Penn wrote it.

The coup de grace was the kid's hat pass, which went something like this: "Ladies and gentlemen, I work very hard at what I do and I take great pride in always coming up with new material for my show. This is the way I make my living. If you can afford it, put something in the hat. If not, your smiles and laughter are enough. Thank you."

I looked at Joe and Johnny and said, "Okay, who wants to tell him?"

Johnny said, "Don't do anything till I get back. I have to run to the rest room."

Joe said, "I'm gonna get something to eat—I'll be right back."

Joe hated confrontation, avoiding it whenever possible. Within seconds I was alone backstage while the un-plumed wretch cleared the stage and deposited his props on a bench. He was sweating, but satisfied; it was a good hat pass. I waited for a few minutes, listened to him chatter on about what a nice crowd it was and how they seemed to like his stuff.

Unable to contain myself, I said, "So how long have you been doing Penn's act?"

"Pardon me?"

"I said 'How long have you been doing Penn Jillette's show?'"

"I don't know what you mean. That's my show; I wrote it."

"Really? Now that would be a coincidence that defies some pretty incredible odds. Every word of that show was taken directly from Penn Jillette's show, the one he's been doing since you were in grade school. Where did you hear it? Did you get a CD and memorize it?"

"I don't know where you're getting that idea, but you're wrong. I wrote every word of that show; it's my material."

I was getting angry. "That's complete and utter bullshit and you know it. Some of us have been around long enough to know where most bits *originally* come from, and your show originally came from Penn. And what you should be thinking about the next time you do it is how many more people just like me are in the audience, knowing where you got it. Because some day, some fan of Penn's who knows where you got it is going to hear you, come up onstage, take your microphone and tell the crowd how much better the show was when Penn did it. Or if you're really unlucky, Penn himself will be walking by, hear his show, and make it very hard for you to ever work again."

He continued to protest and I left. The guy was still doing the show the next day, although none of us were now talking to him. And he's still making a living doing festivals.

You'll know him when you see him. He sounds exactly like Penn Jillette. And he's completely featherless.

25

THE ROUTINES

| Abbott | *Costello, how did you get up in that tree?* |
| Costello | *How did I get up in the tree? I sat on it when it was an acorn.* |

IN THE LATE 1940S, when I was seven or eight and living in my grandfather's house, professional comedy reached my ears for the first time. It came through the large cabinet radio/phonograph in the living room. I'd pull out the radio drawer, turn it on, tune it to the right station, lie down on my back on the carpet and stare up at the glowing tubes. I listened to Jack Benny, Amos 'n' Andy, Bob Hope, and Our Miss Brooks.

I loved Benny and his boisterous cast. His sound-effects laden trips to his vault, his surreal conversations with Dennis Day, and his encounters with the department store floorwalker convulsed me. Benny created a world of characters around him and let them have their moments, much like Seinfeld did fifty years later. He didn't tell jokes or do impressions. But he could get a two-minute laugh from a simple silent reaction, *on the radio*.

My favorites were Edgar Bergen and Charlie McCarthy. Bergen and his dummy were on the air from December 17, 1937 to July 1,

1956. The popularity of a radio ventriloquist, when one could see neither his dummy nor his skill, stumped most critics, then and now.

Even knowing that Bergen provided Charlie's voice, I imagined Charlie McCarthy as a genuine person. The first time I saw a picture of him in his top hat, cape, and monocle, I was startled. Not at all what I had envisioned. Bergen featured other characters, notably the dim-witted Mortimer Snerd and the man-hungry Effie Klinker.

But Charlie was the star, and Bergen always presented him as a precocious child: debonair, girl-crazy, and sharp enough to top the hilarious W.C Fields. It was their testy and hilarious exchanges that stuck with me over the years.

W.C. Fields	*Well, Charlie McCarthy, the woodpecker's pinup boy!*
Charlie	*Well, if it isn't W.C. Fields, the man who keeps Seagram's in business!*

———◆———

W.C. Fields	*I love children. I can remember when, with my own little unsteady legs, I toddled from room to room.*
Charlie	*When was that? Last night?*
W.C. Fields	*Quiet, Wormwood, or I'll whittle you into a venetian blind.*
Charlie	*Ooh, that makes me shutter!*

———◆———

W.C. Fields	*Tell me, Charles, is it true that your father was a gate-leg table?*
Charlie	*If it is, your father was under it.*
W.C. Fields	*Why, you stunted spruce, I'll throw a Japanese beetle on you.*

Charlie	*Why, you bar-fly you, I'll stick a wick in your mouth and use you for an alcohol lamp!*

———————•———————

W.C. Fields	*Step out of the sun, Charles. You may come unglued.*
Charlie	*Mind if I stand in the shade of your nose?*

Bergen's comic timing was perfect. He handled Charlie's snappy dialogue with aplomb. The unique and distinct personalities of Charlie, Mortimer, and Effie made the show crackle with life and laughs. This was Bergen's appeal, the personality he applied to his characters.

Many years later, as Joe and I worked on situations and dialogue that would capture and hold the highly mobile audiences at Renaissance festivals, the echoes of Charlie's sharp-edged exchanges with Fields, Bergen, and the guests on Bergen's show bounced around in my head. Thus, in a swordfight:

PUKE	*Do you yield?*
SNOT	*I have not yet begun to fight!*
PUKE	*THAT'S why I asked.*
SNOT	*Where hast thou been?*
PUKE	*The Crusades. I was wounded thrice at Constantinople, my hose slashed, my doublet cut, my sword hacked like a handsaw.*
SNOT	*Have a scar?*
PUKE	*No thanks, I don't smoke.*

Much of our early material was written in this style – a challenge followed by a clever insult, with a generous dollop of bad puns. We were instinctive actors, with little academic training on our resumes. But we recognized a funny line when we heard one, and we decided early on that whatever made us laugh would suffice for our audiences.

If I could crack Joe up, or vice versa, the crowd might just come along for the ride. And if they didn't, more spectators would show up in an hour. We did five shows a day; there was an abundance of guinea pigs for our little science lab of comedy.

SNOT   [ALONE ONSTAGE] *Friends, Romans, countrymen, lend me your ears!*

PUKE   [BACK OF THE AUDIENCE] *What are you gonna do; make a necklace out of them?*

SNOT   [IGNORING HIM] *To be or not to be, that is the question.*

PUKE   *That's two questions.*

We made sport of expository Shakespearean speeches delivered in staccato bursts by actors we had seen, where it was obvious they were more interested in impressing the audience with their technique than they were in shedding light on the play:

PUKE   *Leicester and Tocester, far from Sussex' eastern hills on Cawdor's border, enjoined are with Russel, Scroup and Sussel, Somerset and Dorset's foe and Bolingbroke of Bedford's enemy.*

SNOT   *Did you hear what you just said?*

PUKE	*I wasn't listening.*
SNOT	*The Crusades are over, you can get parts for your head now.*

But the show was getting tired. The old puns and conceits were predictable and sounded more lame to us every time we walked onstage. The element of surprise was gone. Joe and I were showing up every season, galumphing through our shows, confident that the laughs would be there even though the material hadn't changed much from the year before, or the year before that.

Michael Levin and Peter Simmons wrote a gem of a script that we eventually turned into our third CD, *Puke & Snot's Comical Bum*, and I told Joe it was time to admit that while we might be serviceable comic actors, we certainly weren't writers. We needed new material, and it didn't seem likely it would be coming from us.

Many well-known working comedians over the years had a stable of writers they could depend on for new ideas. While that scenario was financially untenable for us, maybe hiring one good writer to produce a sketch or two per season would freshen up the show and help us give our audiences something new and unexpected. While Michael's *Comical Bum* was excellent; it was a richly plotted film script with a cast of thousands – nothing Joe and I could turn into two-man stage magic.

But Michael was the guy who understood the comedy, the rhythms of two-man dialogue and the necessity of a good punch line every eight seconds. He was a good actor, but an even better writer. In fact, the best sketch writer we knew.

I asked Michael to come up with a seven to ten-minute piece in the same style as his *Comical Bum* script. A couple of weeks later he handed me one of the funniest pieces of two-man comedy I'd ever seen.

Michael Levin, the best comedy
writer you never heard of

Joe and I weren't the quickest ponies in the paddock, but we knew good comedy when we stepped in it. We quickly edited and adapted it to our own personalities, cut some lines, added others and opened our first show that summer in Colorado with "The Magaga Routine," an Abbott & Costello-style sketch that depended for its impact on Snot misunderstanding the meaning of the term "magaga" while Puke tries to teach him the basic elements of bullfighting. It quickly became our signature piece, our "Who's On First."

THE MAGAGA ROUTINE

PUKE   *It was Spain, sir, where I first celebrated the festival of the bull.*

SNOT   *Sounds like you brought some back.*

PUKE   *There I was, alone in the arena, alone with a ferocious bull. My cape over my shoulder, my hat in my hand . . .*

SNOT   *Your breakfast in your shorts.*

PUKE   *My cape over my shoulder, my hat in my hand, and a rose clenched between my teeth.*

SNOT   *Now they won't have to look for flowers when they bury you.*

PUKE   *The rose is for the lovely senoritas. They adore bullfighters.*

SNOT   *They do, huh? Say, how do I get into this bullfighting stuff? I would make an excellent doormat.*

PUKE   *Matador.*

SNOT   *Whatever.*

PUKE   *You?   Don't be ridiculous. You could never be a bullfighter. You don't have the poise; you don't have the stature . . .*

SNOT   *Yeah, but I know where to get a cape.*

PUKE	*There's more to it than that. You must know how to handle yourself properly. You have to be able to walk into an arena filled with thousands of bullfighting fans, look them in the eye, proudly wave your cape at them and say:*
SNOT	[HE IS ABSORBED IN HIS MOVES] *Woolly-bully, woolly-bully . . .*
PUKE	[WHACKS HIM] *Exactly how many other people are in there with you?*
SNOT	*I don't know, but they didn't pay to get in.*
PUKE	*Woolly-bully?*
SNOT	*It was workin' for me.*
PUKE	*So, you think you could be a doormat?*
SNOT	*I know I could.*
PUKE	*All right, I'll teach you everything I know about bullfighting.*
SNOT	*This won't take long.*
PUKE	*So you are the bullfighter.*
SNOT	*I am the bullfighter.*
PUKE	*What's the first thing you do when you enter the arena?*

SNOT	*I get a beer and some nachos.*
PUKE	*No, you acknowledge the crowd.*
SNOT	*Yo, crowd!*
PUKE	*No, not "Yo, crowd!" You salute them!*
SNOT	*Ole. Ole.*
PUKE	*This isn't a Minnesota bullfight; it's ole!*
SNOT	*Oh—the Spanish version . . .*
PUKE	*Yes, the Spanish version. Now if you listen carefully you can hear them, because they are cheering wildly for you! [CROWD CHEERS] Do you know why they're cheering?*
SNOT	*Why?*
PUKE	*Because I'm doing this with my fingers. They're cheering because symbolically, you are fighting the bull for them! You are their hero!*
SNOT	*Yes! Muerto beefo!*
PUKE	*Whatever. So you enter the arena.*
SNOT	*I have entered the arena.*
PUKE	*You salute the crowd.*
SNOT	*I have saluted the crowd.*

PUKE	*Then you reach down and you whip out your magaga.*
SNOT	[PAUSE] *My what?*
PUKE	*Your magaga.*
SNOT	*In front of all these people?*
PUKE	*You take out your magaga and show it to the crowd!*
SNOT	[PAUSE] *They're gonna laugh.*
PUKE	*No, they're gonna cheer.*
SNOT	[SHAKES HIS HEAD] *No, they're gonna laugh.*
PUKE	*You proudly display your magaga and throw it casually over your shoulder.*
SNOT	[LONG PAUSE] *You can do that with your magaga?*
PUKE	*Of course.*
SNOT	*Mine won't go past my hip.*
PUKE	*Well, you do the best you can. Now . . . you bow and you blow a kiss to the queen's box.*
SNOT	*Excuse me?*
PUKE	*It's a sign of respect.*

SNOT   *Not where I come from.*

PUKE   *Well, they do things differently in Spain.*

SNOT   *No kidding. Then what?*

PUKE   *Then you approach and hand your magaga to the Queen.*

SNOT   *Wait a minute! I only met her a second ago.*

PUKE   *That's all right. ALL the matadors do this.*

SNOT   *ALL the matadors?*

PUKE   *Of course. It's another sign of respect.*

SNOT   *Okay. So the queen's got my magaga in her hand. Is the crowd still cheering?*

PUKE   *Absolutely.*

SNOT   *Is the queen cheering?*

PUKE   *Not at all.*

SNOT   *No? Doesn't she like my magaga?*

PUKE   *They're all the same to her.*

SNOT   *If she doesn't cheer, what does she do with it?*

PUKE   *She ties a ribbon around it and hands it back.*

SNOT	*Not too tightly, I hope.*
PUKE	*Enough so it doesn't slip off while you're waving it around. Now the music starts, signifying the bull is about to enter the arena. You take your magaga firmly in both hands . . .*
SNOT	*And run!*
PUKE	*No, you stand firm as the bull makes a pass at you.*
SNOT	*What kind of bull is this?*
PUKE	*A big one. You elegantly evade the pass. Then you make a pass at the bull.*
SNOT	*"Hey Toro, get a load of this magaga!"*
PUKE	*[SWATS HIM] I'm warning you . . . Now, this excites the bull.*
SNOT	*So he IS that kind of bull!*
PUKE	*No! He's an angry bull!*
SNOT	*You'd be angry, too, if a bunch of doormats were waving their magagas in YOUR face all day!*
PUKE	*Never mind that! The bull snorts! He paws the dirt! He flares his nostrils! He charges!*
SNOT	*Gangway!*
PUKE	*And you stick him with your magaga!*

SNOT	*Owww! While he's MOVING?*
PUKE	*It's a skill. It takes practice.*
SNOT	*No doubt.*
PUKE	*The bull is injured!*
SNOT	*He's not the only one.*
PUKE	*The bull falls to the ground!*
SNOT	*And so does my magaga.*
PUKE	*As the bull lies motionless . . .*
SNOT	*I light up a cigarette.*
PUKE	*No, you don't!*

The success of the Magaga routine led to further requests to Michael to come up with new sketches that we could turn into annual gifts to our loyal audiences. We had agreed with the Minnesota festival that we would perform on a new stage in a relatively undeveloped part of the grounds. We acted as bait to lure patrons into the area to see our show, to then wander and shop in the new craft booths that popped up on the east side of the festival.

The new venue was the Cartage, built to resemble the remains of a small ship. Our shows took place on the main deck with the audience gathering on benches under protective sails stretched out above them.

Michael soon came up with another brilliant script, a routine wherein Snot shows Puke how to become a pirate, complete with teaching him the nomenclature of a typical pirate ship. Michael designed it as another Bud and Lou dialogue in which Puke clearly does not comprehend the meaning of a sailor's common vocabulary.

This version of the pirate routine contains two pieces we added later that never seemed to work as well as the rest of the sketch, The "Captain Kidd" segment and the "Never Mind" insert. We've never performed them, other than a quick trial in front of a small audience to see how we liked each one. We didn't.

I'D LIKE TO BUY AN EYE

SNOT	*I myself was once a pirate. A ferocious buccaneer. There was even a price on my head.*
PUKE	*How much?*
SNOT	*Two dollars.*
PUKE	*Why only two dollars?*
SNOT	*I told you, I was a buck-an-ear.*
PUKE	*I don't believe for a minute you were ever a pirate.*
SNOT	*Of course I was. I was known as the "Unhousebroken Dog of the Sea."*
PUKE	*The Unhousebroken Dog?*

SNOT	*I took a ship whenever I felt like it. Haven't you ever heard of Captain Kidd?*
PUKE	*Who was Captain Kidd?*
SNOT	*He was the son of Old Man Kidd.*
PUKE	*Old Man Kidd?*
SNOT	*His father was a pirate also.*
PUKE	*The old man?*
SNOT	*Yes.*
PUKE	*Who was the old man?*
SNOT	*He was a Kidd.*
PUKE	*How could he be a kid?*
SNOT	*The whole family were Kidds.*
PUKE	*The mother and the father?*
SNOT	*They were all Kidds. His grandfather was a Kidd.*
PUKE	*Were his father and his grandfather kids at the same time?*
SNOT	*Of course. They were all Kidds.*
PUKE	*How old was the youngest kid?*

SNOT	*48.*
PUKE	*He was a pretty old kid.*
SNOT	*The older he got, the more of a Kidd he became. He was a desperate man.*
PUKE	*You mean a kid.*
SNOT	*Of course he was a Kidd. Captain Kidd. But he was a man.*
PUKE	*While he was a kid?*
SNOT	*Yeah, he was a Kidd all his life.* [MELODRAMATICALLY] *And when he was old and gray, and ready to die, he called his little grandson to his bedside, and the little grandson looked up at his grandfather's face just before Kidd breathed his last—*
PUKE	*Ohhh . . . the kid was dying . . .* [HE BLUBBERS]
SNOT	*No, the captain was dying.*
PUKE	*Poor kid.*
SNOT	*As he was breathing his last, the little Kidd looked up into old Kidd's face and he said—do you know what he said?*
PUKE	*"Oh you kid. . . ?"*

SNOT   [SMACKS HIM] *He asked him where he had buried his treasure. You see, Captain Kidd loved his only grandson. Do you know why he buried his treasure?*

PUKE   *He was kidding around?*

SNOT   *For his grandson!*

PUKE   *Well, wasn't his grandson a kid?*

SNOT   *Of course he was.*

PUKE   *So he hid it for the kid?*

SNOT   *Yes.*

PUKE   *Did Captain Kidd kid the little kid, or did Kidd ever tell the little kid where he hid it?*

SNOT   *No one knows. He died at the age of 74.*

PUKE   *Too bad. He died so old for such a young kid.*

SNOT   *Yes. But he was one of the most bloodthirsty pirates who ever lived. You'd love the pirate way of life. The riches of the world are at your feet. The women quiver and the ships go down.*

PUKE   *I'd rather have the ships quiver and the—*

SNOT   *Stop that!*

PUKE   *And so would he . . .* [POINTS TO AUDIENCE MEMBER]

SNOT	*But it's not easy! You must pass several tests.*
PUKE	*You have to pass a test to be a pirate?*
SNOT	*That's right.*
PUKE	*So who licenses those guys?*
SNOT	*Oh you think you could be a pirate?*
PUKE	*Of course I could. I got diseases they haven't even heard of yet, I smell bad, I dress terribly, and that guy could be on my crew.* [TO AUDIENCE MEMBER] *We'll start ya off as cabin boy; how's that? Later on we'll make sure ye get a little Captain in ye.*
SNOT	*Okay, Mr. Smarty-Tights,* [GIVES HIM AN EYE PATCH] *put this on. It was left over from my pirate days. It will make the men fear you.*
PUKE	[TRIES IT ON HIS CROTCH] *Great. How do you attach it?*
SNOT	*Not there!*
PUKE	*Oh, it's an eye-patch! Why didn't you say something?*
SNOT	*That will make the men chase you around the ship.*
PUKE	[LAUNCHING INTO FLAMBOYANT PIRATE-ESE] *All right, get your little pirate butts up on deck, we're going to have a flogging! Then we'll sing a few songs from Peter Pan . . . the Richard Simmons pirate fantasy. Hey, a pirate on Wheel of Fortune: "I'd like to buy an eye."*

SNOT	[CUFFS HIM] *Quit fooling around. Is the eye patch securely in place? Now, way in the back, leaning against that tree, there's a guy in a maroon T-shirt. Read what it says on the shirt.*
PUKE	*Okay, I can do that.* [PAUSE] *I can tell you one thing—he's not just leaning against the tree.*
BOTH	*Yechhh!*
PUKE	*Well, it's a festival, what do ya expect?* [LONG PAUSE] *Okay, he's finished.*
SNOT	*So is this bit if you don't hurry up.*
PUKE	*You can't rush good comedy.*
SNOT	*Since when has this crap ever been good enough to do slowly?*
PUKE	*Okay, Okay.* [SQUINTS] *I see the shirt.*
SNOT	*Thank God.*
PUKE	*It looks like an advertisement of some kind. It says: "D.A. Mertz, Urology Clinic. If it hurts when it squirts, talk to Mertz."*
SNOT	*Excellent. You passed the eye test. Now what kind of ship would you like to command?*
PUKE	*Aren't they all the same?*

SNOT	*Not in the least! Would you like a sloop? A brig? A bark? A cutter? A clipper? A ketch?*
PUKE	*Aha! I knew there was a ketch!*
SNOT	*Pick a ship already.*
PUKE	*Aw, frigate.*
SNOT	*No, c'mon, pick one.*
PUKE	*I just did. A frigate.*
SNOT	*Oh. Okay, we'll start you off with a simple frigate with three masts. Now the right side of the ship is starboard. And what's left?*
PUKE	*The other side.*
SNOT	*Port! Left is port! Left, port. Left, port.*
PUKE	*Fine with me. We shoulda left port an hour ago.*
SNOT	*Now assume your command.*
PUKE	*At the front of the boat?*
SNOT	*Bow!*
PUKE	[BOWS]
SNOT	*No, the front of the ship is the bow.*
PUKE	*And that's where I'll be.*

SNOT   *You'll be astern.*

PUKE   *I'll be a stern what?*

SNOT   *The captain stands at the back of the boat!*

PUKE   *Okay, so I'll be standing on the stern.* [MOVES TO STERN]

SNOT   *No, you don't stand on the stern; you stand on the deck.*

PUKE   *The rear deck?*

SNOT   *That's right.*

PUKE   *It is?*

SNOT   *It is.*

PUKE   *I thought starboard was right.*

SNOT   *It is.*

PUKE   *So what's back here?*

SNOT   *Back here is the poop.*

PUKE   [PAUSE] *Excuse me?*

SNOT   *You stand on the poop.*

PUKE   *I'd better be careful where I step.*

SNOT	*No, the whole deck is the poop deck.*
PUKE	*Jeez! What have these pirates been eating?*
SNOT	*What difference does it make?*
PUKE	*I want to know how deep the poop is.*
SNOT	*The poop is several feet above the main deck.*
PUKE	*No kidding?*
SNOT	*Sure. It's designed to be like that.*
PUKE	*And that's where I command from? The poop?*
SNOT	*Yes.*
PUKE	*No wonder the men fear me. Say, suppose I get a collect call from nature. Do I just add to the poop?*
SNOT	*Of course not. You go in your head.*
PUKE	[TRYING TO GRASP THE CONCEPT] *I'm havin' a hard time picturin' that.* [PAUSE] *I can't imagine any position that would be at all comfortable.*
SNOT	*You're a pirate. Comfort is the last thing you worry about.*
PUKE	*Apparently so. Any special reason why I would go in my head?*

SNOT	*You're the captain, right? It's your head, right? You're the only one allowed to use your head.*
PUKE	*So then, the rest of the crew doesn't go in my head?*
SNOT	*Of course not.*
PUKE	*Thank God.*
SNOT	*That would be disrespectful.*
PUKE	*I should say so. Let 'em use their own heads.*
SNOT	*Oh, the crew don't have heads.*
PUKE	*None of them?*
SNOT	*No. They don't need 'em. They're just the crew.*
PUKE	*[PAUSE] How do they see where they're going?*
SNOT	*They go over the side.*
PUKE	*Well, I imagine they would if they can't see where they're going. Isn't there a railing or something?*
SNOT	*Sure, there's a bulwark, but they'll just go over it. You can't stop a pirate from going. You wouldn't want to try, either.*
PUKE	*I suppose not. What kind of crew have no heads?*
SNOT	*Roughnecks.*

PUKE	*Look! Over the horizon!*
SNOT	*Is it a three-masted barkentine?*
PUKE	*No, it's that guy in the maroon shirt!*
SNOT	*It's a Spanish galleon, laden with gold!*
PUKE	*How much gold is in a galleon?*
BOTH	*Two cups in a pint, two pints in a quart . . .*
SNOT	*"Never Mind."*
PUKE	*What?*
SNOT	*The name of the ship: it's the "Never Mind."*
PUKE	*Never mind what?*
SNOT	*The name of the ship.*
PUKE	*What ship?*
SNOT	*"Never Mind."*
PUKE	*Don't you want to tell me?*
SNOT	*I am telling you.*
PUKE	*Are you?*
SNOT	*I told you once.*

PUKE	*I didn't hear you.*
SNOT	*Yes you did.*
PUKE	*Do you mind telling me again?*
SNOT	*Certainly not.*
PUKE	*Well, what's the name?*
SNOT	*"Never Mind."*
PUKE	[PAUSE] *So it's a secret?*
SNOT	*Is what a secret?*
PUKE	*The name of the ship.*
SNOT	*No, it's not a secret.*
PUKE	*Then what is it?*
SNOT	*"Never Mind."*
PUKE	*Well then, keep it to yourself.*
SNOT	*I'm NOT keeping it to myself. I'm telling you.*
PUKE	*Then what's its name?*
SNOT	*"Never Mind."*
PUKE	*Do you know what I'd like to do to you?*

SNOT	*No, what?*
PUKE	*Never mind.*
SNOT	*Wait a minute! It's flyin' the Jolly Roger! It's a pirate ship!*
PUKE	*A pirate ship?*
SNOT	*Aye!*
PUKE	*Bring me my red shirt!*
SNOT	*And why would you request a red shirt?*
PUKE	*Because when I wear my red shirt in battle if I am wounded my men will not see me bleed and they will fight on without me!*
SNOT	*That's noble of you, Puke—but wait! There's not just one pirate ship, I now see TEN pirate ships!*
PUKE	*Ten ships?*
SNOT	*Aye!*
PUKE	[PAUSE] *Bring me my brown pants! Think I'm gonna need 'em?*
SNOT	*Depends. Give your men the order to come about!*
PUKE	*Okay guys, hold hands, form a circle, gather round!*
SNOT	*Tell 'em to trim the sails!*

PUKE	*Cut a couple inches off that one! It looks like crap!*
SNOT	*Aim your cannons at the foremast!*
PUKE	*Aim your cannons at—I thought there were only three masts.*
SNOT	*There are. But the first mast is fore.*
PUKE	*[LONG PAUSE] If the first mast is four, then where's the third mast?*
SNOT	*That's mizzen.*
PUKE	*The third mast is missin'? Where the hell did it go?*
SNOT	*Behind the main.*
PUKE	*The water main? The Spanish main? Charlemagne?*
SNOT	*The main mast.*
PUKE	*What's the main mast?*
SNOT	*Number two.*
PUKE	*I thought poop was "number two."*
SNOT	*The poop is on the rear.*
PUKE	*NOW THAT'S THE FIRST THING YOU'VE SAID THAT MAKES SENSE!*
SNOT	*What's confusing you?*

PUKE	*I wanna know where's the fourth mast?*
SNOT	*There's only three masts!*
PUKE	*Then the fourth is missin'?*
SNOT	*No, the third is mizzen.*
PUKE	*Well I know it's missin', I'm asking you where the hell it is!*
SNOT	*I told you, it's sticking out of the poop!*
PUKE	*Let me get this straight: I'm being attacked by a Spanish vessel, and she's bearin' down hard a-port. That's left. The crew has gone over the right side of the ship, that's starboard, because they don't have heads so they can't see where they're goin'. The Spanish ship's a proud three-masted frigate! I've come about, trimmed my sails, and aimed my cannons. I'm standing sternly on the poop. If my first mast is fore, my third mast is missin', and my main mast is stickin' out of the poop, what do I use to board her with?*
SNOT	*Your dinghy.*
PUKE	*Not on your life, Bucko!* [RIPS OFF PATCH] *Besides, what if my dinghy is mizzen?*
SNOT	*Maybe you forgot to tie it to the stern.*

Our ongoing battle with the Bard

The pattern was set. Puke & Snot's would be a much more traditional and recognizable comic relationship, with Abbott & Costello as their models and guides. Joe's ability to mimic the hilarious reactions and the long, confused pauses of Lou Costello was our biggest asset. I was able to perform straight-man functions quite easily. As long as Michael continued to provide us with the occasional bit of master wordplay, we would be able to keep the show fresh enough to keep audiences coming back. And of course, he did.

His next contribution ended up a lovely combination of his take on a sexually confused band of Merry Men and some material Joe and I had already been doing. This one saves any Bud and Lou wordplay until the end, when Sherwood Forest comes up in the conversation.

SURE WOULD, SHERWOOD

SNOT   *Sir, if you insist on interrupting my performance,
            you'd better hope that England has a blood bank!*

PUKE   *I don't know about that, but I'm pretty sure they've
            got a Liverpool.*

SNOT   *What is it that you do, sirrah?*

PUKE   *I'll tell you what I do. I do what men do, I do what
            men DARE do, I do what men DAILY do not
            knowing WHAT they do . . . da do ron ron ron da do
            ron ron.*

SNOT   *Now come forth and confront me, if you have the
            pith for it!*

PUKE   *You question my pith?*

SNOT   *I challenge your pith!*

PUKE   *I smell an insult!*

SNOT   *It might be your tights. Did you remember to wash
            them out?*

PUKE   *Never mind my tights. We were talking about my
            pith.*

SNOT   *That's why you have to wash them out. Now
            approach, you counterfeit!*

PUKE	*Counterfeit? Sir, I am no counterfeit. To die is to be a counterfeit, for he is but the counterfeit of a man who hath not the life of a man. But to counterfeit dying when a man thereby liveth is to be no counterfeit, but the true and perfect image of life itself.*
SNOT	*Boy, that "Hooked On Phonics" really works.*
PUKE	*Now who be ye, sirrah?*
SNOT	*My name is Thomas Snot.*
PUKE	*Interesting name.*
SNOT	*It's Flemish.*
PUKE	*You know me only as Ralph Puke, but I have gone by many names.*
SNOT	*Yes, I spoke with your ex-wife and several of your names came up.*
PUKE	*Once I was an outlaw, living in the forest.*
SNOT	*Living in the forest?*
PUKE	*Where else would an outlaw live?*
SNOT	*An out-house?*
PUKE	*My name was legend in these parts.*
SNOT	*Big deal . . . parts of me are legendary, too.*

PUKE	*Yeah. He keeps them in a jar. I was known as . . . the Prince of Thieves!*
SNOT	*You mean . . . you are . . .*
PUKE	*Yes . . .*
SNOT	*DRACULA!*
PUKE	*That's the Prince of DARKNESS, you idiot!*
SNOT	*Oh yeah. I was wondering what you were doing out in the daylight . . .*
PUKE	*Y'know, sometimes I look at him and I think "What a sad waste of food and oxygen."*
SNOT	*Okay, okay. Give me a second . . . hey, I recognize the hat . . . you're Kevin Costner! Can I have your autograph?*
PUKE	*No!*
SNOT	*Then I want the six bucks back I dropped on WATERWORLD.*
PUKE	*We all do. I could use a man of your initiative. How would you like to join the Merry Men?*
SNOT	*What's that, a glee club?*
PUKE	*You shall follow my lead. I rob from the poor and give to the rich.*

SNOT   *Don't you mean that the other way around?*

PUKE   *No, I went Republican last election . . .* [BOOS AND
            HISSES] *Well, that divided them up in a hurry.
            With my band of Merry Men, I seek out injustice
            and right what is wrong.*

SNOT   *You don't see anything wrong with living in the
            woods with a bunch of guys who wear tights?*

PUKE   *Come join me, I'll introduce you to "Little John."*

SNOT   [GRABS HIS SWORD] *You try it and I'll introduce
            you to "Mr. Kneecap."*

PUKE   *What's the matter with you? All my men are jolly
            good fellows! Stout! Hearty! and Loyal!*

SNOT   *Yeah, it's just the "merry" part that's got me worried.
            The whole thing sounds a bit unorthodox.*

PUKE   *Nonsense. We have a friar living with us.*

SNOT   *Well, that's good—*

PUKE   *He has us on our knees every morning.*

SNOT   [PAUSE] *He must be Greek Orthodox . . .*

PUKE   *Could be. We call him "Tuck."*

SNOT   *I don't want to know why! What do a bunch of
            outlaws need a priest for anyway?*

PUKE	*He leads us in prayer and song.*
SNOT	*Sounds like YMCA summer camp. What do you pray for?*
PUKE	*We pray that the sheriff doesn't catch us.*
SNOT	*Well maybe you guys should rent a room someplace and stop doing it in the forest.*
PUKE	*What?*
SNOT	*Never mind. Aren't there any women in your group?*
PUKE	*Ah yes, there is Maid Marian.*
SNOT	*A maid? So you guys don't do your own tidying up?*
PUKE	*She's not that kind of maid. She is fair and pure and good.*
SNOT	*You mean a virgin?*
PUKE	*Of course.*
SNOT	*Why am I not surprised? She lives in the woods with your men?*
PUKE	*Sometimes?*
SNOT	*And she's still a virgin?*
PUKE	*Of course!*

SNOT	*Then why the heck is everybody so merry?*
PUKE	*Because we are fighting for a just cause.*
SNOT	*Just cause?*
PUKE	*Just 'cause there's nothing better to do! We are awaiting the return of Richard!*
SNOT	*Who's he, the towel boy?*
PUKE	[TO AUDIENCE] *Well, kids, are ya picking up on this? This is the version of Robin Hood that Mom and Dad rent when you're away at camp . . . no, he's not the towel boy, he's Richard the Lion-Hearted! While he was off fighting the Crusades, his evil brother seized the throne!*
SNOT	*And hocked it?*
PUKE	*No, he's just sitting on it.*
SNOT	*Maybe he's just keeping it warm until Richard gets back?*
PUKE	*No! There is much trouble in the land!*
SNOT	*Yeah, and it sounds like most of it is going on in those woods. This forest you're from wouldn't be named "Gump," would it?*
PUKE	*The location of our forest is a closely guarded secret. Would you like to hear it?*

SNOT	*Sure would.*
PUKE	*Oh, so you know already.*
SNOT	*Know what?*
PUKE	*The name of the forest.*
SNOT	*No, I don't. Would you tell me?*
PUKE	*Sherwood.*
SNOT	[LONG PAUSE] *Okay. When?*
PUKE	*When what?*
SNOT	*When will you tell me the name?*
PUKE	*I just told you the name.*
SNOT	*I must've missed it. Would you tell me again?*
PUKE	*Sherwood.*
SNOT	*Great. Any time you're ready.*
PUKE	*Ready for what?*
SNOT	*Ready to tell me the name.*
PUKE	*I just did.*
SNOT	*You did?*

PUKE	*Sure did.*
SNOT	*Then would you tell me again?*
PUKE	*Sherwood.*
SNOT	*Okay. [PAUSE] I missed it again, didn't I . . . ?*
PUKE	*It's Sherwood! Sherwood Forest! The location of our hideout is Sherwood Forest!!*
SNOT	*Well. I guess it's not a secret anymore, is it?*

Our most recognizable bad joke

Early Puke & Snot scripts depended heavily on our establishing a relationship with a female audience member at some point in the show, allowing us to dig into the arsenal of double entendres we had collected over the years to provoke nervous giggles among the onlookers.

Michael presented us with the coup de grace of all our "romance" segments, an opportunity for Puke to instruct an extremely naive Snot in the art of romance. It became one of our most popular pieces.

SNOT'S ROMANCE LESSON

PUKE *Your problem is you have no tact with women. No sense of romance.*

SNOT *Pish tosh. I beg to differ. I'll never forget my first love. She was beautiful, passionate, everything a man could want.*

PUKE *Did you save the receipt?*

SNOT *Of course.*

PUKE *That's what I'm talking about. Now watch, and learn!* [TO HER] *Your lips are like red wine, I should like to drink from them. Your eyes are like sparkling pools, I should like to bathe in their beauty. Your hair . . . ah, your hair . . . your hair is like a golden field of wheat. I should like to . . . umm . . . cut it, thresh it, and bake it into muffins.*

SNOT *Does the ringing in his ears bother you at all?*

PUKE	*Well, what else can you do with wheat? What else can you do with her hair? How about a fluff, cut, and a perm?*
SNOT	*You stop teasing her!*
PUKE	*I'm not; I'm teasing her hair.*
SNOT	*I'll have you know that woman you're accosting happens to be my sister.*
PUKE	*Right. You don't look anything like her.*
SNOT	*That surprised my father, too.*
PUKE	*Don't give me that. You're not related to her.*
SNOT	*I'm not? [TO HER] Hey, you wanna play worm digger?*
PUKE	*Come here. Stand up here! I'm going to teach you a lesson. Now look. What do you see?*
SNOT	*I see faces.*
PUKE	*A sea of faces.*
SNOT	*That's what I said; I see faces.*
PUKE	*Some beautiful faces.*
SNOT	*Yes, beautiful.*
PUKE	*Some handsome faces.*

SNOT	*Handsome faces.*
PUKE	*Some . . .*
SNOT	*Hairy faces. And whoa! Some ugly faces!*
PUKE	*Well, that's why they stand in the back.*
SNOT	*Is that your neck or a heater hose on a Mack truck?*
PUKE	*Stop that! Concentrate on the beautiful faces! There are many beautiful faces in this audience. Why if all these sweet young things were laid end to end . . .*
SNOT	*I wouldn't be a bit surprised.*
PUKE	*There are many beautiful faces. None, however, that I can see, more beautiful than . . . this! [SELECTS A WOMAN]*
SNOT	*Whooaa! Oh my my, oh hell, yes, time to put on that party dress!*
PUKE	*Hey! Remember, try to keep this in Renaissance mode!*
SNOT	*Right. Forsooth and anon, good mistress, I prithee, and . . . RAMALAMADINGDONG!*
PUKE	*Stop it. Here. Now listen carefully. You must look her in the eye.*
SNOT	*In her eye.*

PUKE	*You must think romance!*
SNOT	*Romance!*
PUKE	*Imagery!*
SNOT	*Imagery!*
PUKE	*Poetry!*
SNOT	*Poetry!*
PUKE	*Sweep her off her feet!*
SNOT	*Fire hose!*
PUKE	*No. Go ahead; give it your best shot. I'll be right here if you need help.*
SNOT	*Your lips are like . . . your lips are like . . .*
PUKE	*Red! Try a color.*
SNOT	*Your lips are like red . . . meat! I'd like to chew on them till I gag!*
PUKE	*This is supposed to be romance, not a trip to the Outback. Keep going.*
SNOT	*Your eyes . . . your eyes are . . . neatly arranged on either side of your nose.*
PUKE	*Great. Otherwise she'd be a Picasso, you moron. Tell her her eyes sparkle with the brilliance of thousands of stars in the summer sky.*

SNOT	*Your thousands of eyes . . .*
PUKE	*No . . .*
SNOT	*Your beautiful eyes throw brilliant shards of light all around . . . you should be hanging upside down in a disco.*
PUKE	*Forget the eyes, move on to something else.*
SNOT	*Your hooters . . .*
PUKE	*Something else.*
SNOT	*Your hair . . .*
PUKE	*Careful, that's where I had problems.*
SNOT	*Your hair is like a field of sun-ripened wheat.*
PUKE	*That's good.*
SNOT	*. . . I should like to run barefoot all over your head.*
PUKE	*I'll have to apologize for him, my dear. He saw a sign that said DRINK CANADA DRY so he went there and did.*
SNOT	*It was two-for-one.*
PUKE	*Well, you've got her in the palm of your hand.*
SNOT	*I wanna get her in the backseat of my car.*
PUKE	*Well don't tell her that.*

SNOT	*Fine. You wanna play wormdigger?*
PUKE	*YOU CAN'T TALK THAT WAY TO A LADY!*
SNOT	*WHEN I SAY IT TO A GUY I GET BEAT UP!*
PUKE	*Stand over here! Learn something for once in your life. If you're going to be romantic, first of all you've gotta be charming!!! I'll bet you ten bucks I can get her to kiss me.*
SNOT	*You're on.*
PUKE	[TO WOMAN] *You wanna make a quick five bucks?*

*Wayne pushing the envelope, our first
album cover*

The Saturday afternoon in September that I selected a stunning blonde who was sitting in the perfect spot, easily accessible on the aisle, as the intended target for Joe's romance lesson was one Joe would never forget. She stood up on the bench, as was customary, and Joe's eyes widened in appreciation. She wore tight jeans, a white tee with the word "Wicked" scrolled across the front, which, it turns out, is the name of a porn production company.

The show was explosively funny, with an ad lib or two from the beautiful subject to keep it rolling along perfectly. As the show ended and we passed the hat, the young man accompanying her asked us if we knew who she was.

I replied no, but it was fun to have had the chance to put her in the show.

"This is Miss October, *Playboy's* latest centerfold."

She chatted with us, insisted on posing for pictures, and introduced us to her parents. A small town Minnesota girl who hit the big-time magazine soft-porn industry – currently dating Michael Keaton, she said, and so happy to meet us.

She returned for our five o'clock show, insisted on taking our names and addresses, and sailed off with her proud parents in her wake. Someone magically produced a copy of the October issue of *Playboy* and, sure as hell, there she was, a teenage boy's instant wet dream, air-brushed to perfection.

A month later, a package arrived at my downtown office, inside were two copies of the October Playboy. A card placed precisely in the centerfold was from the Unclothed One.

It read simply: *Thanks for being a fan.*

I thought about this for a moment, called Joe and told him he received a card – not *from* a fan, but *to* a fan.

26

THE BEDROCK

Reality, while generally probable, is not always interesting.
~ John Hodgman

FROM THE FIRST PERFORMANCES of Mouldy and Wart in 1974 through the summer of 2008 on the ship stage at the Colorado festival, the one consistent thread that ran faithfully through thirty-four years of the Puke & Snot Show was The Remarkable Uniqueness of Joe Kudla.

Renaissance festivals have always attracted a wide variety of eccentric, idiosyncratic souls, creatures with wonderful creative instincts who sometimes team up with like-minded people to create one-of-a-kind performing troupes like Cirque du Soleil, Rogue Oaf and Fool, The Flying Karamazov Brothers, The Flaming Idiots, and Danny Lord. (That duck in his act? Smarter than Danny, really, and much funnier. The duck writes the jokes)

Joe was an Exclusive. Born and raised in northeast Minneapolis, a tight-knit community of Polish and Eastern European immigrant families, Joe was as much at home in the bars, bowling alleys and blue collar neighborhoods of the Twin Cities as he was onstage. When Joe stepped into Arone's Bar on Central Avenue, the whole place welcomed him exactly as the gang at Cheers welcomed Norm.

Joe sat down, a cold draft beer appeared as if by magic, and he would spin tales of bizarre people and events that were unbelievable in their complexity and hilarious in their telling. Those of us who listened to Joe's stories over the many years he entertained us knew that much of what we heard was a product of his storytelling ability and probably not connected to any reality we understood; but it made no difference. The stories were entertaining, and that was the point with Joe.

The fact that Joe became a fine stage actor early on was as much a product of who he was as it was any course of study he engaged in. His whole life was a performance and, as far as I could tell, there was no time he was ever really offstage.

Danny Lord under his writer.

Memorizing a script was simply a matter of telling someone else's story better than they could tell it themselves. Joe listened to a friend relate a tale of exotic adventures, dark treachery and near catastrophic events, and even as the story unfolded you could see him mentally concocting his own fable that would certainly top the one he was hearing.

Radiating an undeniable intensity in every theatrical role he took on, Joe was the one person you watched no matter who else was onstage. I was always too involved with measuring the audience reaction and trying to keep from choking while speaking with a mouthful of masticated carrots to pay much attention to the details of Joe's performances as Snot; but whenever I saw videotape of one of our shows, his reactions to my blustering line readings and his perfectly timed responses to my punch lines always surprised me.

He was, often unintentionally, the funniest stage presence I've ever seen. After many years of watching audiences watch him, I became convinced that one of the main reasons crowds continued to show up in large numbers was that the word was out—the Puke & Snot Show was not to be missed because there was a strangely unbalanced actor in it who could go off at any time. You wanted to be there if it happened.

Joe found it impossible not to show his true feelings, even onstage. If he got frustrated with an audience member, he showed it. If he was upset with me or what I was doing, he let me know. His eyes grew large, his neck muscles stiffened, and the same look passed over his face that was there whenever he hooked his driver into the water.

I am not pleased.

At those times I did my best to distract him as one might attempt to divert a Doberman from attacking the mailman. If I had a bright-shiny object, like say, a sword, I'd wave it at him. Maybe toss him a cookie. Anything to get his mind off whatever he was obsessing about at that moment. He was a dangerous actor, volatile, unpredictable. That unique quality of his brought an edge to our show that often was more interesting than the comedy.

When I first saw him onstage, he was a popular local actor working the best theaters in the Twin Cities. He was a master of dialects, playing Irish laborers, Shakespearean nobility, and Czechoslovakian bureaucrats. I watched him in a production of *Playboy of the Western World* at Theater in the Round, and his memorable portrayal of Christy Mahon, the "hero" whose stories about his life and exploits beguile a whole community, could serve as a theatrical metaphor for Joe's life.

Christy stumbles into Flaherty's tavern, claiming he's on the run because he killed his own father. *Joe's relationships with his father, Joe Sr., and his brother were difficult and sometimes violent.* Christy is a skilled storyteller, and is seen because of it as something of a town hero. *Joe was an equally skilled weaver of tales, and easily convinced the unwary that his exploits were more remarkable than the facts would bear them out to be.* Christy loses Pegeen's love and respect when she finds out that Christy lied about killing his father. *Joe's relationships with women often failed when they realized he had spun some wild stories that turned out to be just that.*

I often thought that Joe saw himself as a contemporary Christy Mahon, a playboy, who traveled his world as a curious visitor, a storyteller whose raison d'être was always to get a reaction from his audience, whether it was another guy on a barstool or a thousand people at a festival.

He gave me an insight into his relationship with his father one afternoon over a cold beer at the end of a long festival day. We were talking about our dads and our memories of good times and bad. Joe said he didn't have a lot of good memories. One of the worst was his high school graduation. When his father handed him an envelope ostensibly containing Joe's graduation gift, Joe opened it, pulled out a piece of paper, scanned it and asked, "What's this?"

"It's your burial plot," replied his smiling father. "Now you won't ever have to worry about buying one. I got you a good spot right there with the rest of the family."

I sipped my beer in silence for a few moments, and finally all I could say was, "Sorry, man. That's really bizarre."

Joe replied, "Yeah, it is what it is."

Joe was a man of many interests and avocations, an avid reader, a musicologist, a sports junkie. We sat backstage and talked about the Twins and the Vikings. He had running bets on football with my son Pat every week during the Minnesota festival. He sat in his truck backstage at the Colorado festival between shows and listened to the Twins broadcasts on satellite radio. I'd hear a knock on my trailer door, open it, Joe would hand me a note or a prop and say, "Twins down 4-1, bottom of the seventh, Bonser's pitching; we're screwed." And he'd leave.

His knowledge of American rock 'n' roll history was legendary. On our many road trips around the country, I could count on Joe to immediately name any singer whose song was playing on the car radio. He not only identified the artist, he gave me a brief Wikipedia-styled history of his or her career.

I'd ask, "Who's that?"

He'd reply, "That's Robert Plant. Before he joined Led Zeppelin he met John Bonham in a band called The Crawling King Snakes. They both went on to play in the Band of Joy; then he met Jimmy Page and joined the Yardbirds, which eventually became Led Zeppelin. I've got all their albums."

I never stumped him, ever.

Joe was resigned to the amusing but annoying fact that nobody could correctly pronounce his last name, especially if it had to be announced in a public forum.

"Good evening, welcome to the Hilton, Mr. Kurdlu."

Airport security agents cheerily sent him through the checkpoint with a "Have a nice day, Mr. Kadla." Or "Mr. Crudela." Or "Mr. Could-lay."

It never failed.

To my wife, Joe was forever "Mr. Toodles." He once described to her how a maitre d' had loudly and cheerfully turned "Mr. Kudla" to "Mr. Toodles" one night when his table was ready at a Las Vegas restaurant. His Christmas cards from our family after that always included Jan's endearing salutation, "Merry Christmas to Mr. Toodles."

I was waiting at the Miami airport to pick up Joe, but I didn't know what flight he was on. I approached an information desk and asked the two women on duty to page my friend and have him pick up a white courtesy phone. I wrote his name on a piece of paper, handed it to the younger one and pronounced it for her.

She picked up the microphone, looked at the name and paused..."Uhh..." she froze.

The older, more experienced attendant reached over, confidently took the slip of paper and said, "I'll take this one." She picked up the microphone and said, "Would Mr. Joe Kidlo please pick up a white courtesy phone. Mr. Joe Kidlo."

I shook my head and looked up to see Mr. Kidlo heading toward me, smiling broadly as if to say, "See? I told ya. Only two syllables. No respect."

The crowning blow, the piece de resistance, the masterwork of mispronunciation occurred one day at the airport in Tampa when the guy in the National rental van pulled up to the drop-off zone, looked at his customer list and asked, "Is there a Mister . . . Radio here?"

Joe glumly shot up his hand and said, "That's me."

I called him Mr. Radio ever after.

Despite these public sleights, Joe was fiercely dedicated to the show and whatever audience showed up, whether it was fifteen hundred people or five. I often lobbied him backstage: we had only a few people out there sitting in the rain, I could make an announcement that the show was cancelled and ask them to come back later. Why waste our energy on a few drunks too stupid to come in out of the rain?

His response was always, "Nah, let's just do it—it's rain or shine; they paid their money. We can do this."

He worked with hangovers, with raging fevers, when he was nauseated and flat on his back, when he was injured, and when most actors would have just called it in. He went onstage and lit it up.

Joe had a comically dark view of the universe and his place in it—he loved being on the road with his CDs playing loud; he enjoyed good food, a good cigar, and an audience for his stories. And he hated technology. He fought it for years.

When I explained one day how easy it was to burn music CDs and mix them for road trips, he finally relented and bought a computer. But he never really learned to use it. He had no patience for the myriad technical problems computers might introduce into his life. Like so many other things, he took his aversion to technology to extremes.

One day during his final summer he stopped in my alley with a few boxes of tee shirts to unload. I looked out my kitchen window and saw him carrying them awkwardly through the access door of my garage. I walked outside and said, "Why don't you open the main door and make it easier?"

He said, "I tried the switch; it doesn't work."

I pressed the big opener button. The door came up and he said, "I hate technology." He had pressed the light switch.

I laughed, "Joe, garage door openers have been around for seventy years."

"It's still technology. I hate it."

I saw him in his last local theatrical performance in 2007 when he played a series of sixties and seventies professional wrestlers at the history theater in St. Paul in a play entitled *The Baron*. It was one of the funniest performances I'd seen in years. Joe did all the voices perfectly: Mad Dog Vachon, The Crusher, Vern Gagne, all of them, in costumes that weren't exactly flattering to Joe's fifty-seven-year-old body—just wearing them demanded a level of courage I've never had.

He spent every performance being tossed around the ring, slammed into posts and konked with metal chairs. The critics recognized him appropriately for that performance. He told me afterwards that the show beat him up physically more than anything he ever did onstage, but he never complained.

When Ron Peluso, the artistic director of the History Theater, told me that Joe was easy to work with, I asked if we were talking about the same Joe Kudla. Later that fall Joe introduced me to the Baron and his wife, who had accepted Joe's invitation to come to the festival and watch the show. We all sat around my trailer afterwards and shared stories of the professional wrestling and festival circuits and the blurry line between show biz and everyday life.

Joe as Mad Dog Vachon: total commitment

27

LOSING SNOT

There is no cure for birth and death save to enjoy the interval.
~ George Santayana

THIRTY-FIVE YEARS have raced by since that first meeting in the red Naugahyde booth at Jimmy Hegg's in downtown Minneapolis. The little show that germinated out of that first seed of an idea has traveled far, entertained thousands and created lasting memories and relationships I cherish.

Joe's final festival performances in Colorado the summer of 2008 were just as full of commitment and energy and dark paranoia as his very first efforts in the straw and dirt of Jonathan, Minnesota, in 1974.

So it was Monday, August 11th; I was in my living room in South Minneapolis complaining to Jan that Joe hadn't called and we were supposed to rehearse later that morning and, damn it, he'd better not be late for this one and all the stuff our Sunshine Boys relationship brought out in me whenever Joe wasn't doing what I thought he should be doing.

My cell phone rang. When I saw Joe's brother Mike's name on my caller ID, something stopped me and for a brief moment I thought about not answering the call. But I did, and the news was both crushing and, strangely, not surprising. Joe had died, his Monday morning running friends found him on his living room floor after he didn't show up for their scheduled run.

I heard later that he had experienced chest pains playing at a local golf tournament on Sunday, but didn't want to bother anyone or check himself into the hospital. The Minnesota festival was opening the following Saturday, and I'm sure he thought that nothing could stop him from being there – that whatever he was feeling was something he could handle.

But he was gone.

I wandered around my house for a long time, trying to process what it meant. I always thought of Joe as indestructible. True, I knew his habits, his diet, his refusal to compromise his lifestyle for a few extra years of "safe" living. He worked out, lifted weights, and ran regularly. But he ate whatever he wanted, stayed at Arone's till closing too many times and refused to consider that guys in their fifties occasionally needed a little preventive maintenance.

I was the guy with the history of cardiac trouble. I had an angioplasty in '96, two more in '07, and I was eight years older than Joe. He had no warnings that I knew about. Joe gone? The son-of-a-bitch. Didn't even say goodbye. So like him. Just take off on his own. I got angry, but only briefly. I remembered what he said whenever we sat around backstage between shows and got philosophical.

We'd be talking about friends who've passed, people we once knew who were no longer walking around on the planet, and Joe said, "When it's time to step out of the canoe, I'll step out of the canoe. No regrets."

This seemed to take care of it for Joe, a simple, direct way of dealing with impermanence. Don't spend too much time worrying about it; live your life, and certainly try to live it so there's nothing to regret when it was finally time for "the dirt bath," as he put it.

But for those of us left behind, it was too soon, Old Boy, too soon. In the flood of correspondence I received after Joe died, a few messages from friends and fans of the show stood out for their clarity and feeling. A guy I never met from the Denver area, Ethan Evans-Hilton, wrote:

> *It seems the year for it. Bernie Mac. George Carlin. And while he may not have been as widely known, Joe, who will always remain chief among those haloed devils that make the day-to-day grind possible. I keep a copy of your discs at my desk at all times as a medicinal compound to lend aid and comfort against disjointed bosses, uncooperative co-workers, and the general lunacy of this spinning ball of dirt.*
>
> *You fine gentlemen lent hand to me in proposing a renewal of vows to my wife in front of the swarthy masses in Colorado. I have yet to figure out an appropriate way to say thank you. And now it seems to Joe at least that opportunity is lost. I'll not soon forget approaching him, sitting at the bar afterward, holding court, chomping on a fat stogie like some highfalutin king of comedy from the Catskills of yore.*
>
> *I have basked and bathed in the mischievous mirth and bawdy buffoonery that is Puke n' Snot for over twenty years. And now one of those stars has fallen out of the sky. I can only hope it landed squarely on the head of some sanctimonious, self-important ass and provided him with a well-needed inoculation of humor.*

A guy named Gordon wrote:

One year I made a mistake. I decided to go do the Texas Renaissance Festival. It was a very poor decision and I hated almost every minute of it. One day when I was feeling particularly down, I happened upon Joe who saw me and asked me what was wrong.

I told him how I was regretting being in Texas and how I wished I was just back home. Except I was stuck. He gave me a pretty decent "hang in there, kid" pep talk. I can't even remember the content of it now, but hell... he took the time to do it. He took the time to give a rat's ass and put up some words of encouragement. That's more than most folks would do.

You checked the price of rat's asses lately? Too bad that a nice guy like Joe gets taken away from the world before we're done with him.

An old friend who grew up with us and the Minnesota festival, Carr Hagerman, one of the most original performers ever to climb into a costume at a festival, wrote eloquently about Joe in an essay he penned for the weekly festival newspaper:

Over the past thirty-five years I've seen these shadows change, because so many of the buildings are gone and the trees that I climbed as a performer when I was fifteen have long since been claimed by the wind and elements. The Chapel, the Gutenberg Press, the Armory, and the Blue Lion Tavern, and many more, deceased relatives fallen into wood fires and dust. Our days, our dances, our shows and schedules intertwine with the light of day, with the shadows that cool and the clear open sky that warms. Our closest companion for these long days are these human shadows that walk with us and stand beside us, tallest in the morning, hidden underneath us when the sun reaches its apex, retiring into the soft whispers of twilight.

But as buildings have fallen and gone, so too have many friends of flesh and blood. Today, on the precipice of another year, I'm thinking about our friend Joe. Like so many buildings and trees that have disappeared and fallen from our midst, he is gone. Joe, who practically grew up here, who set the bar for what nearly every entertainer wanted—to be able to make a successful living doing this work. Joe, who rarely had a bad word to say to anyone. Joe, predictable and certain, a perfect foil for a comedic duo, a blue collar, average working stiff and the kind of guy you wanted to have a beer with, to watch the game with, to just hang out with. Joe, quiet and unassuming, the guy next door...you know... that Joe.

We've lost a friend, and a presence as certain as any building. Of course, the comedy will return to his stage, and the laughter will sooth and celebrate Joe's legacy.

But today, I will walk to the ship stage, as many of us will, to have a few quiet moments to consider our missing friend. Mark will be there, doing what he must do to grieve, running the lines that he and Joe knew by heart, coaxing the audience to find the comedic comfort, and returning to normal, one line at a time.

So, if you stand for just a little while and consider the empty space next to Mark, where there once was a familiar shadow of the perfect foil, there will be the warm and certain light of day rolling itself across the stage. Damn, I'll miss his voice, but as it has and as it must, and as all players know, the whole, damn, show, must go on.

Yeah, I suppose it does. If Jimmy were still around, he'd have the perfect line for Joe's early exit. But I'll leave it to a writer who, though not possessed with Jimmy's ear for a good one-liner, still left a strong body of work in his time.

> *Our revels now are ended. These our actors,*
> *As I foretold you, were all spirits, and*
> *Are melted into air, into thin air;*
> *And, like the baseless fabric of this vision,*
> *The cloud-capped towers, the gorgeous palaces,*
> *The solemn temples, the great globe itself,*
> *Yea, all which it inherit, shall dissolve;*
> *And, like this insubstantial pageant faded,*
> *Leave not a rack behind.*
> *We are such stuff*
> *As dreams are made on, and our little life*
> *Is rounded with a sleep.*

~ William Shakespeare, *The Tempest*

Mr. Radio

Remembering Joe, onstage 2008

28

MY FAVORITE CRITIC

I hope I don't live long enough to find out all my children are stupid.
~ Helen Sieve

FOUR MONTHS BEFORE Joe decided to take early retirement, my ninety-year-old Irish bodyguard beat him to it. My sister Katy called me one April morning to tell me a friend had found mom on the floor of her apartment. She'd suffered a massive stroke and a heart attack. The next four days were spent saying goodbye to the strongest, smartest woman I'd ever known. She'd outlasted Ben by a good twenty-one years, and the celebration of her life commenced.

This was the woman with the spine of steel who shortly after my birth, put me in her dad's '38 Ford and drove from Minnesota to Monterey, California, so her husband Ben could spend a few more days with us before he shipped off to the Philippines; the woman who nursed her aging mother in her home while she ran a restaurant and raised five children; the woman who was more than once the subject of the old joke: What's the difference between mom and a Rottweiler? Eventually, the Rottweiler lets go.

I always knew she was proud of my work. She never liked the Puke and Snot names, but I know she enjoyed talking to her friends about her actor child. She'd sit in the audience at the Minnesota festival and pick her laugh lines carefully. Often, if the joke was a little too risqué for her liking, she'd frown at me and shake her head as if to say, 'Watch it, Buster. You're getting a little too big for your britches.'

I tried to save the best jokes I'd hear in my travels for mom and her friends, picking just the right moment when everyone was in the mood for a little story. A quick glance, a warning, and if she was sitting next to me a sharp elbow in the ribs, would invariably accompany my launching a good joke. She never completely trusted my taste and was deathly afraid I'd embarrass her with something out of bounds. I rarely did.

And I can't remember to this day the story I told her and Edna, her best friend, at a table in my brother Michael's café in Long Prairie many years ago, but they both laughed so hard they spilled their coffee and ended up wiping their eyes and cleaning their glasses, still laughing as we left the restaurant. Very satisfying. I spent years trying to make that happen again.

Joe and I had a line in the "Sure Would, Sherwood" routine that caught Mom's attention one Saturday afternoon. The line occurs when Joe questions me (as Robin Hood) about my lifestyle, "living in the woods with a bunch of guys who wear tights:"

SNOT   *It all sounds a bit unorthodox.*

PUKE   *Unorthodox? Nonsense, we have a friar living with us. He has us on our knees every morning.*

SNOT   *Must be Greek Orthodox.*

PUKE	*No, he's Roman Catholic I believe. We call him Tuck.*

SNOT	*I don't want to know why!*

After we passed the hat and signed some tee shirts, she strolled up with her head cocked the way she always did when she had a question that needed an immediate answer. "How'd you like it, mom?" I asked. She got right to the point.

"Why do you need to say Tuck is Roman Catholic? I don't think you need to bring *that* into it."

"Because it's the setup for the punch line, Mother. It's no big deal. I'm not bashing Catholics."

"I don't think you need it; you should get rid of it."

"Okay, I'll think about it."

Later that night I mentioned to Joe that mom thought she could improve the Robin Hood bit, we chuckled because people were always good-heartedly suggesting jokes they thought we should use, but as the experts on comedy and the most hilarious guys we knew, we would nod patiently, let them have their input, pretend to consider it, then go about our business.

I was vaguely aware, however, that the Tuck line never really got the laugh I always thought it should. Just for fun, I wrote it down without the Roman Catholic reference.

SNOT	*Must be Greek Orthodox.*
PUKE	*Could be. We call him Tuck.*

Eureka! The oldest rule of comedy: tell it in the fewest words possible. The reason the line wasn't getting a big laugh was *there were too many words in the setup.* I told Joe I was going to try something different the next day.

The first show on Sunday morning, Joe fed me the cue, I tried it mom's way, and got the biggest laugh we'd ever had. I called her that evening and told her the Roman Catholic reference was gone and it was now a funnier bit. She was pleased.

Thank you very much, Mother. For everything. Come see me anytime. And give me notes. I promise I'll carefully consider them.

Mom, Dad and me in California, 1943

29

STILL DOWNWIND OF THE ELEPHANTS

*All along the untrodden paths of the future, I can
see the footprints of an unseen hand.*
~ Sir Boyle Roch, Irish member of the British Parliament

ONE NIGHT LONG AGO, I was sitting with Formerly
Fred at Jimmy Hegg's. Jimmy stopped at our table and invited us to
meet and share a meal with one of his old show biz friends who was
in town for a builder's show. Henny Youngman was on his way over
for dinner. He always stopped to see Jimmy whenever he came to
Minneapolis. In fact, he often bought Jimmy's latest jokes and used
them in his show. He arrived alone, came in through the kitchen
from the parking lot, sat down with us, ordered a steak and, for the
next forty-five minutes, gave us a free show.

Fred and I had most of Jimmy's one-liners at the ready along
with a few of our own, but Henny was having none of it. More than
once, after Fred tossed off a pretty good comeback, Henny put down
his knife and fork and said, "Hey, I'm the professional here. I do the
jokes; you're the audience."

We asked him what he was doing in Minneapolis at a builder's
show.

"In this business, when they call you and they have a check, you show up."

He was well into his sixties, still sharp and energetic, with perfect timing and command of the room. At one point, two obviously impaired middle-aged women appeared, stood on either side of his chair, and started flirting. Henny was a gentleman for a few minutes, then suddenly pulled his napkin out of his shirt, tossed it on the table and said, "Okay, ladies, let's cut to the chase. What are you doing later? Would you like to come to my hotel room after the show?"

The women beat a quick retreat, stammering something about having to get back to their husbands. Henny replaced his napkin, picked up his fork and said, "That's the way you handle *that*."

Years later, Joe and I were driving in Pennsylvania. A large sign outside a shopping mall proudly announced: TONIGHT AT THE SUSQUEHANNA MALL – ONE SHOW ONLY – HENNY YOUNGMAN. He was still showing up.

———◆———

What's the best thing about being the oldest act at a Renaissance festival? No peer pressure.

Renaissance festivals still pack 'em in. The idea that began in California in the sixties has a firm hold on the public imagination. You can find little versions of the old established faires in just about every state in the country.

New talent has replaced the original artists who found their first audiences in the straw and mud of faux English villages from New York to Texas. Rogue, Oaf and Fool have moved on, as have the Ratcatcher and Pastorius. Penn & Teller have paddled into the mainstream; you can see them everywhere. Many other former headliners are quietly living out their years at The Merrie Prankster's Retirement Home and Lawn Dart Community south of Punta Gorda, Florida.

But you can still see veteran, professional shows like the slick and slightly twisted Johnny Fox, the hilarious silent artist Arsene Dupin, Terry Foy as Zilch the Torysteller, Lloyd and Rosie Brant as the Wacky Chickens, Hilby the Skinny German Juggle Boy, and Ded Bob and Smuj, the funniest two-on-one encounter you'll ever experience.

An insider's must-see tip? Mitch Cohen, The Turtle Man, runs the driest, silliest half hour of melodramatic turtle racing and color commentary ever to grace a ring of hay bales, while Hey Nunnie Nunnie, two lovely and subversive Brides of Christ, remain as shocked, *shocked* at their own material as you are entertained by it.

Worthy descendants of The Great Sven and Professor Lumberti, all of them.

You will always see raw new acts trying to find their audience and their timing. Be patient, they'll figure it out, or they'll go back to whatever they were doing before they decided that working weekends in the heat, humidity, and occasional downpour was a sterling idea.

Getting laughs is an addictive pastime. Once you do it successfully, it's something you want to repeat until you perfect it. Like golf. You hone it, fine-tune it, polish it, but you never perfect it. Every audience is different. Some require a little prodding and others demand the battle cry: "Sons of Norway!"

The startling loss of Joe was a heavy blow, still felt by our families and the thousands of fans who have returned year after year to laugh along with us and share the silliness.

But the literal meaning of "renaissance" is renewal, rebirth. Today the challenge is to shine a new light on old sketches and routines. Snot "Junior" helps me do that. John's ability to deliver a familiar line in a way that makes me hear it differently is an unexpected opportunity to create new laughs for new audiences.

Our little show was never designed for stages beyond a Renaissance festival. We created it for a particular time and place, for an audience who wanted a show that didn't take itself too seriously. As I watch performers like Mick Jagger and Bob Dylan still selling out stadiums, the fact that I continue do a show that requires me to trot around in tights becomes not so much a source of embarrassment as a challenge to finally, with one more audience, perfect it.

ACKNOWLEDGMENTS

A WEEK AFTER THE 2008 FESTIVAL season ended late in October in Crownsville, Maryland, John Gamoke called me and said, "You have to write a book." He'd just returned from ten weeks of the best theatrical relief pitching ever recorded, stepping in and performing brilliantly as Thomas Snot, Jr. after Joe died. John had heard the stories, seen the outpouring of affection for Joe, and told me to get cracking on a book.

I thought about it for a few days, sat down and started to write. Most of it was finished in a month. I left town for a couple of weeks to write about Joe, and ended up in San Diego strolling through Balboa Park where we had done some memorable shows in the 80's. That helped. But I would never have started this without John's insisting there was a story here. Thanks, Gamok.

Special thanks to the hard-working crew at Two Harbors Press. Mark Pitzele was an invaluable guide through the thickets of the publishing process, and Jenni Wheeler, young enough to be my granddaughter but a knowledgeable veteran when it comes to the mysteries of book design. Marly Cornell provided vital editing help, re-working parts of this book where I had hit the wall. Thanks also to Maureen Smith, who took the first draft and pronounced it readable.

Huge thanks to Michael Levin, Wayne Walstead, Daryl Person, Gary Parker, the whole extended Jules Smith family, and dozens more whose names I'll remember the day after this comes off the press.

Thanks to Jim Paradise, who gave us the second biggest compliment we ever got; to Nick in Wisconsin, Karla in Kansas City, and Maryanna in Colorado, who gave us shelter; to Betty, Dave, Rook, Gary, Carolyn, Don Staples, Steve Hedrick, Scott Novotny, Johnny Fox (who still shares his stage with us in Maryland), Arsene, Todd "Monkey Boye" Menton, Joe Leach, Charlie the ProdAss, Peter Moore, Jon Schumacher, the late great Dick Kohl, Eileen, Devon, Andy, Ben, John, Tom, Lucy, Angela, Sal and Linda Garcia, and our good friend and roadie Denny, all of whom were there when I needed them and on whose backs our little show was carried.

And thanks to Al and John, the best poker-playing singing executioners on the planet, who were there with us in the olde days and still break me up with "English Country Garden." And to George Herman the Most Royal, our friend and confidante from day one, thanks!

To the hundreds of thousands who were there every weekend, and to my wife Jan and formidably talented sons Pat and Pete, who were there every day, and who never laugh when I'm not funny and rarely when I am, thank you.

Finally, I am so grateful to my father and mother, Ben and Helen, for their long and productive lives and their love and inspiration. I am unbelievably fortunate to have had them in my life.

ABOUT THE AUTHOR

MARK SIEVE IS AN ACTOR, producer, and director, and the co-creator of the longest-running two-man comedy duo in the country: the Renaissance vaudeville team of *Puke & Snot*. A headline show at festivals and comedy clubs coast to coast in North America since 1974, the act has produced four comedy CDs, a DVD, and a movie script.

Sieve is a graduate of St. John's University in Minnesota, and began his acting career in Twin Cities' theater. He once turned down a professional baseball contract with the Minnesota Twins, and to this day has no regrets.

In addition to the *Puke & Snot* show, seen at festivals from June through October each year, Sieve has appeared in more than fifty theatrical productions, including a production of *Pure Confidence* at Mixed Blood Theater in Minneapolis. In 2009, the play took Sieve off Broadway to the 59E59 Theater in Manhattan.

Sieve is the owner of CIC Productions, a creative entertainment company with offices in the Twin Cities. He has two sons, Pat and Peter, and lives with his wife Janis, their dog, and cat in South Minneapolis.